Children's Adjustment to Adoption

Developmental and Clinical Issues

David M. Brodzinsky
Daniel W. Smith
Anne B. Brodzinsky

Volume 38
Developmental Clinical Psychology and Psychiatry

SAGE Publications
International Educational and Professional Publisher
Thousand Oaks   London   New Delhi

For information:

SAGE Publications, Inc.
2455 Teller Road
Thousand Oaks, California 91320
E-mail: order@sagepub.com

SAGE Publications Ltd.
6 Bonhill Street
London EC2A 4PU
United Kingdom

SAGE Publications India Pvt. Ltd.
M-32 Market
Greater Kailash I
New Delhi 110 048 India

Printed in the United States of America

Library of Congress Cataloging-in-Publication Data

Brodzinsky, David.
  Children's adjustment to adoption: Developmental and clinical
issues / by David M. Brodzinsky, Daniel W. Smith, Anne B.
Brodzinsky.
    p.   cm. -- (Developmental clinical psychology and psychiatry ;
v. 38)
  Includes bibliographical references (p.) and index.
  ✓ISBN 0-7619-0515-4 (cloth: acid-free paper). -- ISBN
0-7619-0516-2 (pbk.: acid-free paper)
    1. Adoption--Psychological aspects. 2. Adopted children-
-Psychology. 3. Adjustment (Psychology) in children. 4. Child
development. I. Smith, Daniel W. (Daniel William), 1965- .
II. Brodzinsky, Anne Braff, 1940- . III. Title. IV. Series.
HV875.B76 1998
155.44'5--dc21   97-45404

99 00 01 02 03   10 9 8 7 6 5 4 3 2

Acquiring Editor:	Jim Nageotte
Editorial Assistant:	Fiona Lyon
Production Editor:	Diana E. Axelsen
Editorial Assistant:	Denise Santoyo
Typesetter/Designer:	Rose Tylak

Children's Adjustment to Adoption

This book is to be returned on
or before the date stamped below

UNIVERSITY OF PLYMOUTH

EXMOUTH LIBRARY

Tel: (01395) 255331
This book is subject to recall if required by another reader
Books may be renewed by phone
CHARGES WILL BE MADE FOR OVERDUE BOOKS

Developmental Clinical Psychology and Psychiatry Series

Series Editor: Alan E. Kazdin, Yale University

Recent volumes in this series . . .

CONTENTS

INTRODUCTION
TO THE SERIES

Interest in child development and adjustment is by no means new. Yet, only recently has the study of children benefited from advances in both clinical and scientific research. Advances in the social and biological sciences, the emergence of disciplines and subdisciplines that focus exclusively on childhood and adolescence, and greater appreciation of the impact of such influences as the family, peers, and school have helped accelerate research on developmental psychopathology. Apart from interest in the study of child development and adjustment for its own sake, the need to address clinical problems of adulthood naturally draws one to investigate precursors in childhood and adolescence.

Within a relatively brief period, the study of psychopathology among children and adolescents has proliferated considerably. Several different professional journals, annual book series, and handbooks devoted entirely to the study of children and adolescents and their adjustment document the proliferation of work in the field. Nevertheless, there is a paucity of resource material that presents information in an authoritative, systematic, and disseminable fashion. There is a need within the field to convey the latest developments and to represent different disciplines, approaches, and conceptual views to the topics of childhood and adolescent adjustment and maladjustment.

The Sage series **Developmental Clinical Psychology and Psychiatry** is designed to serve uniquely several needs of the field. The Series encompasses individual monographs prepared by experts in the fields of clinical child psychology, child psychiatry, child development, and related disciplines. The primary focus is on developmental psychopathology, which refers broadly here to the diagnosis, assessment, treatment, and prevention of problems that arise in the period from infancy through adolescence. A working assumption of the Series is that understanding, identifying, and treating problems of youth must draw on multiple disciplines and diverse views within a given discipline.

The task for individual contributors is to present the latest theory and research on various topics, including specific types of dysfunction, diagnostic and treatment approaches, and special problem areas that affect adjustment. Core topics within clinical work are addressed by the Series. Authors are asked to bridge potential theory, research, and clinical practice, and to outline the current status and future directions. The goals of the Series and the tasks presented to individual contributors are demanding. We have been extremely fortunate in recruiting leaders in the fields, who have been able to translate their recognized scholarship and expertise into highly readable works on contemporary topics.

In this book, David M. Brodzinsky, Daniel W. Smith, and Anne B. Brodzinsky examine *Children's Adjustment to Adoption: Developmental and Clinical Issues.* The authors place adoption in historical context to address issues that affect both the process and outcome of adoption for children and their parents. Theoretical perspectives on the adoption process, along with supportive research, are carefully delineated. Extensive coverage is given to the research on both the adjustment of children and parents to adoption itself and the psychological development, including adjustment and maladjustment, over the course of childhood and adolescence. Children whose adoption emerges from such circumstances as child abuse, parental drug abuse, and parent HIV are also discussed. Adoption across racial and cultural lines and the circumstances such adoptions raise are also examined. The book is excellent in its coverage of theory and research on children and families and the contextual issues pertinent to the adoption process. Clinical vignettes punctuate key points. Assessment and intervention with children and families are also covered. The authors have made major research contributions over the years in understanding the effects of adoption. This book stands as yet another significant contribution.

Alan E. Kazdin, Ph.D.

PREFACE

Every book has a history. Ours began with a question posed by one of us (A. B.) to another (D. B.) some 20 years ago: "What does a young child understand about being adopted, and how does that understanding change over time?" This simple question became a catalyst for an initial research project that in turn led to a series of studies altering the course of our careers. Since the late 1970s, we have been exploring the psychology of adoption, both from research and clinical perspectives. Although most of our work has focused on the development and adjustment of adopted children, we have also studied and worked clinically with adult adoptees, adoptive parents, and birth parents. Overall, we have nearly 50 years of combined experience in this area.

As psychologists, we have often experienced a certain isolation from our colleagues in our study of adoption. In fact, with the exception of behavior geneticists, who are interested in adoptive families primarily in relation to questions concerning the heritability of behavior and psychological traits, only a handful of psychologists in this country are actively pursuing programmatic research on developmental and clinical issues in adoption. Perhaps this is because adoptees represent such a small percentage of the population of children. Perhaps it is because adoption is too closely tied to the field of social work and social service practice. Maybe it is because adoption is seen as a solution to a set of problems and not a potential problem itself. Whatever the reason, relatively few research or clinical articles on adoption appear in psychological journals each year, and until recently, issues related to adoptive family life were seldom represented in edited volumes or textbooks on the psychology of the family.

One of the primary reasons we decided to write this book was to stimulate interest among developmental and clinical psychologists with regard to the study of adoption. Although a considerable amount of interesting and very relevant research has been generated by investigators in other disciplines, especially in the fields of social welfare and psychiatry, it is our belief that the unique perspectives and methodologies associated with psychological research have much to contribute to efforts at understanding patterns of adjustment in adoptees, adoptive parents, and birth parents. Given that adoption is now seen as influencing members of the adoption triad across the entire course of their lives, it seems obvious that developmental psychologists, in particular, would have much to offer to the study and understanding of adoption. Unfortunately, developmentalists have yet to discover this fact. We hope that by raising interesting theoretical, empirical, and clinical questions in this book and by bringing together what is currently known about developmental and adjustment issues in adoption, we will spark greater curiosity among our research and clinical colleagues.

Finally, over the course of our work in this field we have had the support of a number of organizations that we would like to acknowledge. First, we wish to express our appreciation to the National Institute of Mental Health, the Charles and Joanna Busch Memorial Fund of Rutgers University, the Research Council of Rutgers University, and the Division of Youth and Family Services of New Jersey for funding our research and clinical projects. We also wish to thank the many adoption agencies, adoptive parent support groups, and adoption attorneys around the country that have worked with us in the course of research. Finally, we are most appreciative of the time given to us by the thousands of adopted children, adult adoptees, adoptive parents, and birth parents whom we have met and worked with over the years. It is through their generosity in sharing with us their own unique adoption experiences that we have gained our insight into the psychology of adoption.

1

HISTORICAL AND CONTEMPORARY PERSPECTIVES ON ADOPTION

The American family has undergone many dramatic changes over the past half century. In fact, there is so much diversity in the structure and functioning of families today that the so-called traditional family—children living in an intact family with two biological parents—has lost a great deal of its meaning. At present, a minority of children will reside continuously with both of their biological parents from birth until emancipation in young adulthood (Okun, 1996). Some youngsters will experience parental death while still in childhood; many others will be subjected to parental separation and divorce. Some children will live in step families, others with single parents. An increasing number of youngsters will grow up in households headed by same-sex couples; others will be conceived by assisted reproductive techniques and will grow up in families where they have a biological connection to only one, and perhaps neither, of their parents. Some children will live for part of their childhood in foster homes, too often because of neglect or abuse at the hands of biological parents. Still other children will be placed for adoption soon after birth or when they are older. Many of these adopted children will come from other countries or will be of a racial or ethnic background different from that of their adoptive parents and siblings.

Diversity in family life has raised some important questions about the influence nontraditional parenting has on children (Lamb, 1982; Okun, 1996). What is the impact on children of growing up in a household with only one, as opposed to two, parents? Do mothers and fathers each play a unique role in the lives of their children? What impact does early parental loss have on children's development? Does the nature of the loss make a difference? Are children at a disadvantage when they are raised by parents with whom they do not share a biological connection or the same racial or ethnic heritage? How do children fare when they are raised by gay or lesbian parents? Despite the obvious relevance of these questions for developmental theory as well as for social policy and child rearing, relatively little empirical work has focused on developmental and clinical issues related to nontraditional family life, with the possible exception of the impact of divorce on children (Okun, 1996).

This book focuses on one particular form of nontraditional family life: adoption. Our goal is to provide the reader with an overview of research and theory on the development and adjustment of adopted children. We examine developmental outcomes in traditional adoptions—children placed as infants—as well as outcomes involving children with special needs, children placed internationally and interracially, and children living in open adoption arrangements. Finally, we also examine some common assessment and clinical issues that emerge in the treatment of adopted children as well as specific clinical interventions that have been used to help youngsters cope with adoption-related problems.

No book can cover all aspects of a given topic. Ours is no exception. Space limitations require that we restrict our discussion primarily to the psychology of adopted children, not adopted adults, adoptive parents, or birth parents. Readers interested in these topics should consult A. Brodzinsky (1990), Brodzinsky, Schechter, and Henig (1992), Reitz and Watson (1992), Sorosky, Baran, and Pannor (1978), or Winkler, Brown, van Keppel, and Blanchard (1988). Before examining the theoretical, empirical, and clinical literature on adoption, we provide the reader with an overview of historical and contemporary trends in adoption policy and practice.

HISTORICAL PERSPECTIVES ON ADOPTION

Virtually all the major ancient societies—Egyptian, Chinese, Indian, Greek, Roman—practiced some form of adoption. Even the Bible frequently mentions adoption—the most well-known example being the adoption of Moses by Pharaoh's daughter. However, unlike contemporary adoption practice, which focuses on the best interests of the child, historically adoption was primarily a vehicle for meeting the needs and interests of adults and society in general (Benet, 1976; Sokoloff, 1993). For example, adoption was commonly used in earlier times to ensure inheritance lines and the continuity of the family, to fulfill requirements for religious practices involving ancestor worship, to meet requirements for holding public office, to secure additional labor for the family, to ensure maintenance and care in one's old age, and to strengthen alliances between separate, and potentially rival, social groups. In addition, adoption in early societies focused almost exclusively on male adults. Few women or children were adopted during ancient times.

Development of Adoption Law
and Practice in the United States

English common law is often cited as the cornerstone from which much of American law is derived. This cannot be said for adoption law in the United States. Because of the historical emphasis on inheritance rights through blood lineage in England, it was not until the early part of this century that the first adoption statutes were enacted in Great Britain. Thus, as our North American ancestors struggled to deal with the growing problem of homeless and dependent children during colonial and post-colonial times, there were no legal or social precedents within the English system of law and society to guide the development of adoption practice. Instead, a number of social practices, including indenture, placing children in homes for domestic service, apprenticeships, and the emergence of almshouses were used for the care of dependent children who could not live with their biological families.

The first adoption statute in the United States was passed by the Massachusetts legislature in 1851. Interestingly, its provisions are quite similar to those found in most state adoption laws today. The early Massachusetts law required that (1) biological parents consent to the adoption; (2) the child give consent if over 14 years of age; (3) a joint petition for adoption be filed by the pre-adoptive parents; (4) the court find the adopters fit and able to raise the child; (5) the adoption be approved by the court; and (6) all legal rights and obligations of the biological parents regarding the child be severed and transferred legally to the adoptive parents. In the ensuing years, many states followed the lead of Massachusetts and passed statutes governing the practice of adoption. However, it was not until 1929 that all states had developed some form of judicial supervision regarding adoption.

Early adoption law did not require that adoption records be sealed or that access to the records be denied except for good cause. In fact, it was quite common for biological parents and adoptive parents to know one another. In 1917, however, the State of Minnesota passed legislation that resulted in the sealing of adoption records. Over the next 20 years or so, the other states followed suit, and adoption statutes were amended, leading to the sealing of adoption records. For the first time in United States history, birth parents and adoptive parents were legally prevented from meeting one another and sharing identifying information. The child's original birth certificate was sealed under court order and a new, amended birth certificate was issued identifying the adopters as the child's parents. Secrecy and anonymity became the cornerstones of adoption practice. In the 1920s and 1930s, a growing interest in adoption emerged in this country. There was particular interest in newborn babies. The focus on babies grew out of the drop in the birth rate following World War I and the influenza epidemic in 1918, and was facilitated by the development of formula feeding—thereby eliminating the need for a wet nurse. Infant adoption was also supported by the emerging perception that environment, as well as heredity, was important in shaping the child's growth and development.

Unfortunately, the growing demand for adoptable infants opened up many opportunities for unscrupulous individuals seeking to benefit from the misfortune of others. Unregulated "baby brokers" were quite common during this period. Children were often placed in homes with little or no concern about where the child came from, whether the biological parents had given proper consent to the placement, or whether the adopters were fit to parent the child. In response to these abuses, states began to strengthen their adoption statutes, ensuring that proper consent be given by all parties and that potential adoptive parents be investigated. The responsibility for monitoring placements and ensuring that all provisions of the adoption statutes be followed fell on the shoulders of adoption agencies.

Following World War II, the demand for healthy, adoptable infants grew rapidly. Fear of unknown hereditary problems, however, led adoption agencies to keep infants in selective foster homes—called "study homes"—for the first 6 to 12 months of life, so that their physical and psychological development could be monitored. Children with known medical, neurological, and/or psychiatric problems in their background were considered unadoptable at the time (Cole, 1985).

By the mid-1950s, the demand for children began to exceed the number of infants available for adoption. In response, agencies developed highly restrictive criteria for placing children with families. Individuals had to meet a number of questionable social, financial, and psychological standards before being accepted as adoptive parents. The rigidity of adoption agency practice did not go unchallenged for long, however. Demands for reform of the entire child welfare system, including the practice of adoption and foster care, emerged from a variety of sources. In 1955, the Child Welfare League of America held a National Conference on Adoption (Shapiro, 1956). What emerged from the conference was a new focus on casework practice, which, in conjunction with a number of major societal changes beginning in the 1960s and extending into the 1970s (e.g., the civil rights movement, consumerism, the women's movement, changes in social mores and family structure, passage of the Freedom of Information Act, and growth of public interest law firms), set the stage for modern adoption practice (Cole & Donley, 1990).

CURRENT OPTIONS AND TRENDS IN CONTEMPORARY ADOPTION PRACTICE

Currently, prospective adoptive parents have two types of adoption to choose from: agency adoption and independent (nonagency) adoption. The primary difference between these two types of placement is the method by which birth parents give their consent to adoption (McDermott, 1993). In both public and private agency adoption, birth parents legally surrender their child to the agency, which in turn, consents to the adoption by specific parents. In contrast, in independent adoption, birth parents give their consent directly to the adoptive parents.

Data on the incidence and prevalence of adoption in the United States are limited, primarily because the federal government has not systematically collected such data for some time. The most recent year for which national statistics are available is 1986, during which a total of 104,088 adoptions occurred. Of these adoptions, slightly less than one half involved placement of children with nonbiological relatives. Approximately 39% of these latter adoptions were processed through public agencies, 29% through private adoption agencies, and 31% through independent adoption placements. Forty-eight percent of these adoptions involved infants, nearly 26% involved older children and those youngsters with special needs, and 16% were international placements (National Committee for Adoption, 1989).

It is estimated that approximately 2% to 4% of children in the United States are adopted (Bachrach, 1986; Stolley, 1993). Of these youngsters, slightly more than one half are adopted by family members and stepparents; the remaining children are adopted by individuals with whom they share no biological connection. Most of the research on adoption has focused on the latter group of individuals.

The demographics of children who are being adopted has changed considerably over the past 40 years (Stolley, 1993). Since World War II, most children placed for adoption have been healthy, white infants, born to women who conceived prior to marriage. In fact, data from the 1982 National Survey of Family Growth indicate that 88% of all infants placed for adoption were born to never-married women, 6% to previously married women, and 6% to currently married women (Bachrach, 1986). However, growing societal acceptance of single parenthood over the past three decades, coupled with the ready availability of contraception and abortion, has led to a substantial decrease in the number of healthy babies available for adoption. For example, the percentage of unmarried women who chose to relinquish their infants for adoption rather than parent them declined from approximately 9% prior to 1973 to closer to 2% by 1988 (Bachrach, Stolley, & London, 1992). The decline in infant relinquishment was accounted for primarily in terms of fewer numbers of white babies being surrendered for adoption (19% of all premarital births for 1952-1973 versus 3% for 1982-1988). In contrast, unmarried African American women have consistently shown a relatively low level of infant relinquishment (1.5% for 1952-1973 versus 1.1% for 1982-1988).

As the number of infants available for adoption has declined, prospective adoptive parents have chosen to adopt privately, outside of the public and private adoption agency systems. This process, which is legal in all but six states (Connecticut, Delaware, Massachusetts, Michigan, Minnesota, and North Dakota), involves direct contact between prospective adoptive parents and birth parents. In these adoptions, birth parents give their consent for adoption directly to the adoptive parents. Today, more infants are being placed for adoption through independent means than through adoption agencies (Stolley, 1993).

In addition to private adoption, a growing number of individuals and couples are looking beyond the borders of the United States in their efforts to adopt children. Intercountry adoption began soon after World War II and escalated dramatically after the Korean War. Approximately 10,000 children per year have been adopted from other countries by United States citizens in the past few years, the majority of these youngsters coming from Pacific Rim countries, Eastern European countries, and from Central and South America (Stolley, 1993). Most of these children are infants and toddlers; some, however, are older children. In a great many cases, these adoptions involve placements across racial lines.

Domestic transracial adoption has been another source of children for individuals seeking infants and toddlers. Typically, this practice has involved white couples adopting non-white children—usually African American, Latino, and Native American children, or children of mixed racial background. Domestic transracial adoption has declined since the 1970s, however, as a result of opposition from the African American and Native American communities. Still, the practice of placing children outside of their own racial group continues and has recently been affirmed by the federal government through new legislation (Public Law 104-542) that prohibits race from being a barrier to timely placement of a child for adoption.

In 1980, the federal government passed the Adoption Assistance and Child Welfare Act (Public Law 96-272). This landmark legislation sought to create permanence in the lives of children in foster care by establishing guidelines ensuring a timely return to the biological family, or, when this goal was impractical, placement in a nurturing adoptive home. The assumption underlying permanency planning was that adoption offered children greater stability and more long-term benefits than they could hope for lingering in the foster care system (Barth & Berry, 1988). One outcome of this legislation has been the emergence of a large number of children available for adoption. The vast majority of these youngsters are characterized by "special needs" that historically have been barriers to adoption. Most special needs children are beyond the infancy and toddler stage. Many have been subjected to neglect, physical abuse, sexual abuse, and/or multiple foster placements. Too often they have well-developed emotional or behavioral problems, developmental delays, and/or medical problems. Sometimes they are members of a large sibling group. Many are of minority racial status (Rosenthal, 1993). The relatively few infants available through special needs adoption programs frequently have a history of exposure to drugs and/or alcohol during the prenatal period (Barth, 1993). In addition, a growing number of special needs infants entering foster care, and eventually being adopted, are the offspring of HIV-infected women (Levine & Stein, 1994). A sizable percentage of these infants are, themselves, HIV positive.

As a group, those individuals seeking to adopt children are also becoming much more heterogenous than in the past. Traditionally, adoption agencies employed a variety of screening standards to identify suitable prospective adoptive parents. As a result, most adoptive parents in the past were middle-class to upper-middle-class, married, white, infertile couples, usually in their late 20s to early 40s and free of any significant health problem or disability. In contrast, older individuals, unmarried individuals, fertile couples, individuals from lower- and working-class backgrounds, gays and lesbians, disabled individuals, and foster parents were seldom approved for adoptive parenthood by evaluating agencies. During the past 15 to 20 years, however, adoption policy and practice have moved in the direction of "screening in" applicants as opposed to "screening them out." Casework practice is now focused on identifying those individuals or couples who have the ability and motivation to meet the unique needs of children who are waiting for an adoptive home, regardless of marital status, income level, fertility status, race, sexual orientation, and so forth. Adoption agencies have come to recognize that most screening criteria used in the past were rather arbitrary and of questionable value, and that too many individuals who were rejected in the evaluative process were, in fact, valuable but unrecognized and underutilized parenting resources. Today, most barriers to becoming an adoptive parent have been eliminated, greatly increasing the diversity in the structure of adoptive family life.

Another dramatic change in adoption practice that is affecting the lives of children as well as their adoptive parents and birth parents, is the emergence of open adoption (Baran & Pannor, 1993; Berry, 1993). As noted previously, before the early part of this century, it was common for adoptive parents and birth parents to know one another. With the emergence of the adoption agency system in the 1920s and 1930s, however, the practice of adoption became increasingly confidential. The practice of confidential adoption continued unabated until the 1970s, when, in response to a growing outcry from adult adoptees and some birth parents about the damage done to them by the secrecy of the closed adoption system, agencies began to offer clients the option of open placements, in which birth parents and adoptive parents could meet and share identifying information, and if they desired, develop plans for ongoing contact following the adoption placement. The practice of open adoption, which is the focus of much controversy and debate (Baran & Pannor, 1993; Berry, 1993; Kraft, Palombo, Mitchell, Woods, & Schmidt, 1985a, 1985b; Kraft, Palombo, Woods, Schmidt, & Tucker, 1985; Melina & Roszia, 1993), has grown considerably in the past 20 years, further increasing the complexity of adoption practice and the variability within the adoption triad kinship system.

SUMMARY

Adoption has a long and rich history. Beginning as a somewhat informal practice focusing on the needs and interests of adoptive parents and society in general, adoption has emerged in contemporary society as a formalized social service practice, regulated by state law, and geared primarily toward meeting the "best interests of the child." Adoption is also characterized today by greater diversity in the characteristics of children being adopted as well as those individuals adopting them. In addition, secrecy, anonymity, and confidentiality as hallmarks of adoption practice are giving way to greater openness within the adoption system. In short, adoption has become a remarkably varied and complex social service practice, making it difficult to talk about the "average" adopted child or "average" adoptive family. Thus, generalizations made in this book, and elsewhere, regarding adoption must be interpreted with caution. Although we seek to find commonalities among different types of adoption, we also must be sensitive to the high degree of variability that exists in this form of family life.

2

THEORETICAL PERSPECTIVES ON ADOPTION ADJUSTMENT

The past 30 years have witnessed a growing interest among researchers and clinicians in the study of adopted children and their families (Brodzinsky & Schechter, 1990). Much of the literature has focused on the question of whether adopted children are at increased risk for psychological and academic problems compared with their nonadopted peers (Brodzinsky, 1993; Wierzbicki, 1993), as well as on developmental issues and individual difference factors in patterns of adoption adjustment (Brodzinsky, 1987; Brodzinsky, Schechter, & Henig, 1992). Other investigators have focused on psychological issues involving adoptive parents and/or the nature and functioning of the adoptive family system (Kirk, 1964; Reitz & Watson, 1992). A problem that has plagued much of the empirical research on adoption to date is that it has been largely atheoretical. There have been few attempts to collect data systematically in the context of well-articulated theoretical perspectives. Consequently, our understanding of the basis for psychological risk in adoption, as well as the variability in adoption adjustment, is somewhat limited. Although a number of conceptual approaches have been brought to bear on the issue of adoption adjustment, until recently they have been somewhat narrow in focus or have been difficult to test empirically. In the present chapter, we will review some of the more important theoretical models that have been used to understand developmental processes and adjustment patterns in adopted children and their families. A review of the empirical literatures on adjustment outcomes in adoption will be presented in Chapters 4 through 7.

BIOLOGICAL PERSPECTIVES

One approach to understanding adjustment problems in adopted individuals focuses on the role of heredity (Cadoret, 1990). The primary assumption of this perspective is that not only is the development and manifestation of various psychological and behavioral characteristics of human beings strongly genetically determined, but also the relative psychological risk associated with adoption is, in part, genetically based. In other words, it is assumed that the genetic background of children whose parents place them for adoption is less optimal than the genetic background of nonadopted peers. This vulnerability, in turn, is thought to be an important contributor in the increased psychological risk associated with adoption.

There can be no question at this time that heredity plays a major role in the development and manifestation of many psychological and behavioral traits, including various forms of psychopathology (Cadoret, 1990). It is also clear that there is greater similarity in many traits such as intelligence, personality, and even interest patterns between adopted children and their biological relatives compared with adopted children and their adoptive family members (Cadoret, 1990; Grotevant, Scarr, & Weinberg, 1977; Horn, 1983; Loehlin, Willerman, & Horn, 1985). What is still unknown, however, is whether the biological parents of adopted children are more prone to genetically based personality and learning problems, which in part could account for the greater difficulties reported for these youngsters. In support of this position, one study reported that unwed mothers whose children were placed for adoption scored higher on a number of clinical scales on the MMPI than did mothers from a control group (Horn, Green, Carney, & Erickson, 1975). To the extent that the problems measured by these scales have a genetic component—as the researchers suggested—it could be argued that the findings support the position that adoptees generally come from less optimal hereditary backgrounds. On the other hand, even if genetics does prove to play a prominent role in the explanation for the increased adjustment problems of adoptees, it is also important to recognize the obvious role played by the rearing environment in the lives of these children. This point is well made by Scarr and Weinberg (1976, 1983), who note that, although the similarity in various psychological traits between adoptees and their biological relatives is stronger than between these children and their adoptive family members, the rearing environment clearly affects the development and adjustment of adoptees and often leads to higher than expected outcomes compared with controls who come from background environments similar to those of the biological family (Scarr & Weinberg, 1976, 1983).

Another set of factors influencing the biological integrity of adopted children are those experienced prenatally. Adverse prenatal experiences such as heightened maternal stress, poor maternal nutrition, inadequate prenatal medical care, and fetal exposure to alcohol, drugs, and other teratogenic agents are known to be implicated in postnatal developmental delays and childhood behavior problems (Kopp, 1983). Given that many of these complications are more often found among young, unwed mothers (Ward, 1991), including those who place their babies for adoption, it is reasonable to suggest that the adjustment problems of adopted children may be linked, in part, to these prenatal difficulties (Bohman, 1970; Everett & Schechter, 1971; McRoy, Grotevant, & Zurcher, 1988).

Clearly, there is much to be done to unravel the relative contributions of genetics and adverse prenatal experiences, compared with environmental factors, in the development and adjustment of adopted children.

PSYCHODYNAMIC THEORY

Efforts to understand the adjustment of the adopted child from the perspective of psychodynamic theory have a long and rich history and have centered primarily on the unconscious conflicts of adoptive parents and their children, which can distort not only individual development but parent-child relationships (Brinich, 1990). Some authors have focused on the unconscious and unresolved conflicts toward parenthood in adoptive parents, especially the mother (Deutsch, 1945; Toussieng, 1962) and on the defective feelings and disappointments that accompany infertility (Blum, 1983; Schechter, 1970). The deep psychic pain and narcissistic wounds experienced by infertile parents are believed to be re-encountered when the adoptee begins to explore his or her feelings about the birth family (Brodzinsky, 1997; Kirk, 1964). In addition, feelings of envy about the emerging sexuality and fertility of the pubescent child are believed to distort the infertile parents' interactions with their youngster.

The potential confusion for the young child in having two sets of parents with whom to identify also has been linked to adjustment difficulties in adoptees, especially when adoption revelation occurs prior to the resolution of the Oedipal conflict (Wieder, 1977). In addition, the possibility of adjustment problems associated with overreliance on the splitting defense, in which one set of parents is seen as "good" and the other as "bad," frequently has been raised. Psychodynamic writers also have emphasized the difficulty in resolving object loss and the potential conflicts in forming a stable and well-integrated ego identity as complications in the adoptee's psychological adjustment (Brinich, 1990; Nickman, 1985; Sorosky, Baran, & Pannor, 1975).

Despite the absence of strong empirical support for many of the psychodynamic assumptions regarding adoption, the theory continues to inform clinical and casework practice with adoptees, adoptive parents, and birth parents in very meaningful ways.

ATTACHMENT THEORY

The concept of attachment, as originally proposed by Bowlby (1969, 1973, 1980) and subsequently elaborated by many others (e.g., Ainsworth, Blehar, Waters, & Wall, 1978; Bretherton, 1987; Main, Kaplan, & Cassidy, 1985; Sroufe & Waters, 1977), has been conceptualized as an organized behavioral system whose purpose is to foster a sense of security for the infant by maintaining proximity to caregivers, as well as by providing the youngster with a secure base from which to explore the environment. As the attachment system develops, a "goal-corrected partnership" is said to emerge between child and caregivers, which regulates the youngster's *felt security,* especially in times of stress, and leads to more generalized representational models of self, others, and self-other relationships. Furthermore, these internal working models form the basis for the child's beliefs about the competence and worthiness of the self, as well as about expectations regarding whether others will be available to the self as sources of nurturance and support.

Attachment theorists have suggested that early parent-child bonds are the cornerstone for healthy psychological adjustment, affecting development not only in infancy and childhood but in adulthood as well. This assumption has been overwhelmingly supported by empirical research. Children characterized by greater security in their attachment relationships have been found to manifest more positive patterns of adjustment across a host of domains than those youngsters with various forms of insecure attachments (see Cicchetti, Toth, & Lynch, 1995 for a recent review of this literature). Moreover, research also suggests that internal attachment organizations from childhood are related to adult attachment patterns, which in turn affect adult adjustment and behavior, including quality of parenting (Crittenden, 1988; Main & Goldwyn, 1984).

A number of adoption theorists have discussed the potential importance of attachment theory for understanding patterns of adjustment among adopted children and their families, especially for those children placed for adoption beyond the first year of life, as well as those youngsters who experience multiple changes in caregivers or neglecting or abusive rearing conditions, prior to their adoptive placement (Fahlberg, 1979; Johnson & Fein, 1991; Steinhauer, 1983). For example, two early studies by Yarrow and his colleagues found that *all* adopted infants in their sample who were removed from their biological parents after 6 months of age suffered a variety of social-emotional difficulties, and that 10 years later, many of the children still showed some relationship difficulties (Yarrow & Goodwin, 1973; Yarrow, Goodwin, Manheimer, & Milowe, 1973). Research by Tizard and her colleagues (Tizard, 1977; Tizard & Hodges, 1978; Tizard & Rees, 1975) documented the long-term impact of early adverse rearing on the attachment patterns of children who were subsequently adopted. The researchers noted that at 2 years of age, adopted infants who had initially been raised in institutions were more clinging and diffuse in their attachments compared with nonadopted infants. Furthermore, greater social and emotional difficulties continued to be observed in these children when they were 4 and 8 years of age. In contrast to these studies, a more optimistic view of the ability of adoptees to attach to their parents is found in the research by Singer, Brodzinsky, Ramsay, Steir, and Waters (1985). These investigators noted that, when placed within the first few months of life, intraracially adopted infants were able to form attachments to their mothers that were as secure as those formed by nonadopted infants, although interracially adopted infants tended to be somewhat more insecure than their nonadopted counterparts.

Attachment theory has also been used by researchers to examine patterns of adoption stability versus adoption disruption in families with children who were preschool age or older at the time of placement (Barth & Berry, 1988). Findings indicated that children's attachment behaviors that were indicative of growing security (e.g., ability to be comforted by parents, showing spontaneous affection, caring about whether the parents approved of them) generally increased over time for those youngsters whose adoption placements remained stable. Conversely, children who were eventually removed from the adoptive home prior to legal finalization of the adoption showed a decline in attachment-related behaviors over time.

Although the implications of attachment theory for understanding adjustment in adopted children are considerable, relatively little work has been done in this area, especially on the way in which meaningful relationships become internalized in the mental and emotional lives of adopted children as they get older. Research has documented that, when children begin to understand the meaning of their adoptive status, they spend a great deal of time fantasizing about their birth parents and the circumstances of their relinquishment (Brodzinsky, Singer, & Braff, 1984; Smith & Brodzinsky, 1994, 1997).

Clinically, it is common to observe adopted children developing well-articulated, fantasy-based relationships between themselves and members of their birth family, which in turn, affect their adjustment within the adoptive family. Recent advances in attachment theory, emphasizing the role of representational models of self-other relationships, should prove valuable for understanding this aspect of adoption adjustment as well as other adoption-related issues, including whether or not the individual, as an adult, is motivated to search for birth family members.

SOCIAL ROLE THEORY

The publication of *Shared Fate,* David Kirk's (1964) social role analysis of the adoptive family kinship system, is now seen as one of the pivotal points in the development of modern adoption theory and practice. It was the first systematic attempt to explain adoption adjustment in terms of family interaction patterns. A core assumption of the theory is that adoptive family relationships are built, in part, on a foundation of loss—for the adoptive couple, it is the loss of fertility and the desired biological child; for the adoptee, it is the loss of his or her birth origins. In addition, Kirk argues that adoptive parents experience increased stress in relation to the additional tasks, challenges, conflicts, and role incongruities associated with adoptive family life. To cope with adoption-related issues, parents usually adopt one of two primary strategies. Some parents tend to deny, minimize, or reject the meaningfulness of their loss or the differences associated with adoption. Others are better able to acknowledge their loss and the challenges of adoptive family life. Kirk suggested that the acknowledgment-of-difference approach was much more conducive to positive adjustment in the child, since it presumably allowed the youngster greater freedom and opportunity to explore adoption-related issues openly and nondefensively with parents. Conversely, the rejection-of-difference approach was thought to create a rearing environment that inhibited open communication about adoption and reinforced in the child the idea that to feel different is to be deviant.

Empirical support for Kirk's theory, at least in its original form, is limited, especially regarding the link between adoptive family attitudes and communication patterns concerning adoption and children's adoption adjustment. Although some research has found that open communication styles about adoption are associated with more positive adjustment in adoptees (Stein & Hoopes, 1985), other research has found the opposite pattern (Kaye, 1990). Recently, several writers have offered modifications of Kirk's theory to account for the discrepant findings (Brodzinsky, 1987; Kaye, 1990; Talen et al., 1997). In essence, these authors have suggested that problems in adoption adjustment are associated with extreme communication patterns in either direction. In other words, adoptive parents who strongly deny differences or who overemphasize differences in family discussions about adoption are more likely to create an atmosphere that increases the risk for dysfunctional family interactions. In contrast, moderate levels of acknowledging adoption-related differences are assumed to facilitate more optimal adoption adjustment.

Despite the lack of strong empirical support, Kirk's theory has had an important influence on adoption policy and practice. For example, much of the emphasis on openness in adoption today, both in terms of opening sealed adoption records and the creation of open adoption placements, can be traced to the underlying assumptions of this theory.

FAMILY SYSTEMS THEORY

A number of writers, operating within the broad framework of family systems theory, have begun to explore the way in which adoption alters traditional family structure and functioning (Butler, 1989; Reitz & Watson, 1992; Schaffer & Lindstrom, 1990; Talen & Lehr, 1984). Much of this work is closely related to issues originally raised by Kirk (1964, 1981). At the core of this approach is the assumption that adoption creates "a new kinship network that forever links those two families [biological and adoptive] together through the child, who is shared by both" (Reitz & Watson, 1992, p. 11). Within this perspective, the resolution of adoption-related issues and the development of healthy family relationships are believed to be tied to a host of family structural and process variables, including

1. the type of expectations that family members have about how adoption is likely to influence family functioning;
2. the way family members communicate about adoption issues;
3. how families handle boundary issues determining the child's dual connection to two families;
4. how family members cope with potentially sensitive issues related to family loyalty, family secrets, and family customs and rituals;
5. the ability of family members to support one another regarding adoption-related loss; and

6. the success with which the family is able to negotiate the potentially conflicting processes of family integration (i.e., building family connections) and differentiation (i.e., fostering appropriate separateness and individuation among family members).

Although this approach has been extremely useful for conceptualizing clinical issues and treatment strategies in working with adoptive families, to date, it has not generated much empirical research.

STRESS AND COPING THEORY

Although each of the perspectives described above offers valuable insights into children's adoption adjustment, they are, by their very nature, somewhat narrow, focusing primarily on selected factors such as the biological background of the child, attachment relationships, intrapsychic processes, and/or family systems issues. Adjustment to adoption, however, is very complex and highly variable from one person to another. To capture the complexity of this adjustment process, one must approach it from a multidimensional perspective, with an emphasis on both developmental and contextual factors. Recently, several researchers have independently offered similar multidimensional models of adoption adjustment based primarily on stress and coping theory (Barth & Berry, 1988; Berry, 1989-1990; Brodzinsky, 1990, 1993; Pinderhughes, 1996). The model described by Brodzinsky (1990, 1993) will be used to highlight the major points shared by most of these investigators (see Figure 2.1).

Stress and coping theory suggests that when a person views a situation in his or her life as meaningful to the self, but also as potentially threatening, stigmatizing, involving loss, or unduly challenging, a pattern of negative emotions associated with stress (e.g., confusion, anger, sadness, anxiety, embarrassment, shame) is likely to be experienced (Lazarus, 1991; Lazarus & Folkman, 1984). Once the situation is appraised as stressful, various coping options are considered, and one or more eventually activated. Some of these coping behaviors involve attempts to resolve the dilemma through direct action or by redefining the importance of the situation in relation to the self (cognitive-behavior problem solving) or by seeking help and support from others (assistance seeking), whereas other coping behaviors represent attempts to avoid dealing with the stressor by minimizing it or putting it out of one's mind (cognitive avoidance) or by distancing oneself from it (behavioral avoidance). Although no one pattern of coping is always associated with

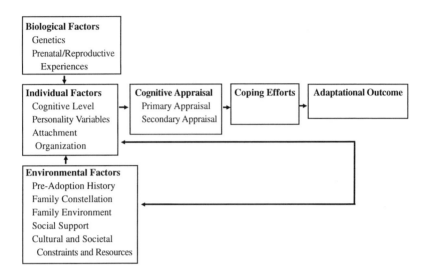

Figure 2.1. A Stress and Coping Model of Adoption Adjustment

more positive adjustment, research generally suggests that overreliance on avoidant strategies, especially in relation to controllable stressors, is often tied to increased adjustment problems (Lazarus, 1991; Lazarus & Folkman, 1984).

A core assumption of the stress and coping model of adoption adjustment is that adoption is inherently associated with a variety of loss- and stigma-related experiences and hence is potentially stressful for children. For example, adoptees experience the loss of birth parents and extended birth family; loss of status; loss of ethnic, racial, and genealogical connections; loss of feelings of stability in the adoptive family; and loss of identity (Brodzinsky, 1990). The degree to which children experience adoption-related stress, though, and the success they have in coping with it, are highly variable. For some children, adoption is appraised in a rather benign or positive way that produces little distress, whereas for other children, being adopted is associated with feelings of confusion, sadness, anger, embarrassment, and shame. When these emotions are experienced, a variety of coping options are considered, and eventually one or more is chosen to reduce feelings of distress. Some children are likely to seek help from their parents, siblings, or friends when they are upset. Others are likely to avoid situations that remind them of adoption or to put all thoughts about adoption out of their minds. Still other children may chose to redefine the relinquishment by the birth parents in a more positive light. The model assumes that problem-focused strategies and assistance-seeking strategies generally are more effective in handling adoption-related distress than avoidant strategies.

Influencing the adoption appraisal process, and ultimately children's adjustment, are a host of child-related resource variables, the most important of which are the youngster's cognitive level, temperament, self-esteem, sense of mastery and control, and relationship security. Thus, it is not until children begin to understand the meaning and implications of adoption—around 5 to 7 years of age—that one expects to see the emergence of sensitivity to adoption-related loss and stigma as well as a shift toward more ambivalent feelings about being adopted (Brodzinsky, 1990; Brodzinsky et al., 1984). Similarly, children with more difficult temperaments, greater self-esteem problems, including diminished self-efficacy and greater relationship insecurity, are expected to appraise being adopted in more negative ways and to have greater adjustment problems.

The current model also recognizes the role of genetics, prenatal and reproductive experiences, and various environmental and interpersonal variables in the adoption adjustment process. These factors are considered contextual variables that are indirectly related to the child's adoption adjustment through their impact on the developing self-system and the cognitive appraisal process. Thus, children whose birth parents suffered from biologically based forms of psychopathology would be considered at greater risk for post-placement adjustment problems. So too would children who experience more prenatal and reproductive complications. Finally, adverse societal and cultural attitudes about adoption, diminished social support for dealing with adoption, adverse rearing experiences in the adoptive family, and a history of adverse preplacement experiences (e.g., multiple foster homes, neglect, abuse) are also assumed to increase the child's risk for maladjustment.

Recent efforts to empirically test the stress and coping model of adoption adjustment have been encouraging. Smith and Brodzinsky (1994) found that the majority of children between 6 and 17 years of age viewed being adopted as somewhat stressful, as defined by ambivalent feelings and intrusive thoughts about their adoption. Furthermore, it was found that 14- to 17-year-olds were more ambivalent about being adopted than either 6- to 9-year-olds or 10- to 13-year-olds. On the other hand, it was the youngest children who were most likely to experience intrusive thoughts about being adopted. These researchers also reported that negative and ambivalent feelings about adoption were positively correlated with both cognitive and behavioral avoidant coping strategies, whereas children's intrusive thoughts about adoption were associated with more approach coping behavior such as problem solving and assistance seeking. In a second study, Smith and Brodzinsky (1997) examined how 8- to 12-year-old adopted children appraised, coped with, and adjusted to the loss of their birth parents. Results indicated that, although children generally had a more positive than negative view of their relinquishment, they still experienced some distress over the loss of birth parents. Furthermore, children who reported higher levels of negative affect about birth parent loss also reported higher levels of depression and lower self-worth. In addition, greater curiosity and preoccupation regarding birth parents was associated with increased externalizing symptoms, as rated by parents. Finally, children who utilized more behavioral avoidant coping when dealing with adoption-related distress displayed greater self-reported anxiety and parent-rated externalizing behavior (e.g., aggression, acting out, etc.), whereas problem-solving coping was associated with increased social competence.

Although still in the early stages of model building and model testing, the work of Brodzinsky and his colleagues (D. M. Brodzinsky, 1990, 1993; Smith & Brodzinsky, 1994, 1997), Barth and Berry (1988), Berry (1989-1990), and Pinderhughes (1996) underscore the potential heuristic value of stress and coping theory for understanding children's adjustment to adoption.

SUMMARY

Numerous theories have been offered to explain the adjustment of adopted children and their parents. To date, most have been rather narrow in focus or have not generated a programmatic study of adoption-related issues. More recent advances in model building in this area have emphasized the multidimensional, developmental, and contextual nature of adoption adjustment [see also the work of McRoy, Grotevant, and Zurcher (1988)]. These conceptual approaches reflect the belief that human behavior is determined, not by a single causative factor, but by the interplay of multiple influences in the context of a developing person and an ever-changing environment.

3

ADOPTIVE FAMILY
LIFE CYCLE

The concept of the family life cycle has been used by theorists to describe the orderly sequence of developmental changes that the family system undergoes over time (Carter & McGoldrick, 1980). This process involves the emergence of unique patterns of family structure and functioning that serve as the focal point for family interaction and contribute to the development and adjustment of family members. In addition to its strong developmental focus, family life cycle theory is inherently contextualistic and based on a interactionist perspective of family life. In other words, it assumes that the family is influenced by the broader sociocultural system within which it exists, and that a dynamic interplay occurs among family members, with parents and childen strongly influencing the behavior and adjustment of one another.

In recent years, a number of adoption theorists have found the family life cycle concept useful for describing the way in which adoption-related tasks emerge over time and interact with the more universal tasks of family life (Brodzinsky, 1987; Brodzinsky et al., 1992; Brodzinsky, Lang, & Smith, 1995; Hajal & Rosenberg, 1991). Furthermore, these writers have suggested that adoptive parents and their children each have their own unique adoption-related tasks, and that the way in which these individuals cope with, and resolve, their respective tasks determines, in part, the adjustment of the adoptive family system. Among the many tasks experienced by parents are those associated with coping with infertility and the transition to adoptive parenthood, discussing adoption with their child, creating a family environment that supports the child's exploration of adoption issues, helping their child cope with loss, supporting a positive self-image and identity in their child in relation to adoption, and in some cases, as the adoptee moves into adolescence and adulthood, supporting their child's plans to search for birth family. Children, on the other hand, do not begin to cope with adoption-related tasks until they know that they are adopted—usually in the preschool years. Over time, they will come to understand what being adopted means, explore their dual connections to two families, cope with adoption-related loss and stigma, attempt to integrate adoption into their emerging identity, and in some cases, make plans to search for additional information regarding their origins and possibly make contact with birth family members. Table 3.1 highlights the various adoption tasks for parents and children at different stages of the family life cycle.

PRE-ADOPTION PERIOD

Most adults, when they get married, plan to have children. Few of these individuals expect ahead of time that there will be difficulties in conceiving a child. Yet, approximately one in six couples will experience a fertility problem (Mosher & Pratt, 1991). When this happens, most couples seek a medical solution, with nearly 50% eventually able to have a child biologically (McEwan, Costello, & Taylor, 1987). The remaining couples must decide whether to remain childless or to seek parenthood through some other means, including adoption.

Because of the societal and personal significance of procreation, the decision to adopt a child is rarely an easy choice. Complicating this decision is the profound stress typically associated with infertility, which often results in both short-term and long-term psychological problems, including heightened feelings of anxiety, guilt, shame, anger and depression; diminished self-esteem; and marital difficulties (Epstein & Rosenberg, 1997; Lieblum & Greenfeld, 1997).

Confronting infertility and eventually deciding to adopt a child is a complex process requiring numerous changes in personal identity and role enactment (Brodzinsky, 1997; Brodzinsky & Huffman, 1988; Daly, 1988, 1989). A primary task for prospective adoptive parents is gradually letting go of the biological parenthood identity in preparation for taking on the identity of adoptive parent. At the heart of this process is "working through" the deeply personal and painful experience of infertility. Although it is unlikely that infertility is ever completely resolved, it is important for the individual or couple to find a comfortable way of incorporating this painful loss into a healthy and functional sense of self. Failure to do so increases the chances that adoptive parents will have difficulty, not only with feelings of entitlement to their child, but with establishing a caregiving environment that supports

TABLE 3.1
Family Life Cycle Tasks of Adoptive Parents and Adopted Children

Age Period	Adoptive Parents	Adopted Children
Pre-Adoption	Coping with infertility Making an adoption decision Coping with the uncertainty and anxiety related to the placement process Coping with social stigma associated with adoption Developing family and social support for adoption decision	
Infancy	Taking on the identity as adoptive parents Finding appropriate role models and developing realistic expectations regarding adoption Integrating the child into the family and fostering secure attachments Exploring thoughts and feelings about the child's birth family	
Toddlerhood and Preschool Years	Beginning the telling process Coping with anxiety and uncertainty regarding the telling process Creating a family atmosphere conducive to open adoption communication	Learning one's adoption story Questioning parents about adoption
Middle Childhood	Helping child master the meaning of adoption Helping child cope with adoption loss Validating the child's connection to both adoptive and biological families Fostering a positive view of the birth family Maintaining open communication about adoption	Mastering the meaning of adoption Coping with adoption loss Exploring thoughts and feelings about birth parents and the relinquishment Coping with stigma associated with being adopted Maintaining open communication with parents about adoption Validating one's dual connection to two families

(continued)

TABLE 3.1 Continued

Age Period	Adoptive Parents	Adopted Children
Adolescence	Helping the adolescent cope with ongoing adoption-related loss Fostering positive view of the birth family Supporting the teenager's search interests and plans Helping the adolescent develop realistic expectations regarding searching Maintaining open communication about adoption	Integrating adoption into a stable and secure identity Coping with adoption loss Exploring thoughts and feelings about birth family and birth heritage Exploring feelings about the search process Maintaining open communication with parents about adoption

normal parent-child relationships as well as success in meeting the challenges of stage-specific adoption-related tasks (Brodzinsky, 1997; Brodzinsky et al, 1995).

Most infertile individuals prefer to adopt an infant, either through an adoption agency or independently with the aid of an attorney. As they proceed with their adoption plans, the couple begins to experience a variety of challenges that are different from those experienced by others in the transition to parenthood (Brodzinsky & Huffman, 1988). Prospective adoptive parents must seek help and rely on others in their pursuit of parenthood. Furthermore, they must undergo a "homestudy" to ensure that they will be able to meet the needs of a child. Although current social casework philosophy views the homestudy as an educative and supportive process, many prospective adoptive parents continue to feel the historical *evaluative* legacy of this practice, which often increases their anxiety and undermines their self-confidence. Many adoption agencies and private adoption attorneys are also offering birth parents the opportunity to choose the family that will adopt their child. In such cases, birth parents are provided with packets of information about a number of prospective families, from which they make their selection. They may also be able to meet, and share identifying information, with the prospective adoptive parents. Although it is believed that this practice increases the birth parents' sense of control and emotional well-being, our clinical experience suggests that it often has an unintended, although typically short-lived, negative impact on adoptive parents. Specifically, many individuals and couples feel as if they are marketing themselves to birth parents, which increases their anxiety and reduces their sense of control. Moreover, when time passes and they have not been chosen by a birth parent for an adoption placement, couples may begin to question their own suitability to be adoptive parents. When a match finally has been made, however, contact with birth parents appears to have more benefits than drawbacks for both adoptive and biological parents (Grotevant & McRoy, 1998).

The transition to adoptive parenthood is also characterized by a more uncertain time frame than is biological parenthood. Once conception occurs, biological parents know that their baby will be born in approximately 9 months. The certainty of the time frame allows them and their support network to plan more effectively for the transition to parenthood. Prospective adoptive parents, on the other hand, have no such time frame. After years of failing to conceive a child, couples apply to an adoption agency or seek out the help of an adoption attorney, and then begin to wait for a child. For some, the waiting period will be quite short—perhaps only a few months. For others, however, it may be years before they have a child placed with them for adoption. The uncertainty of the waiting period often fosters increased anxiety, confusion, feelings of helplessness, and depression among prospective adoptive couples. In fact, it may lead them to question their entitlement to be parents.

Another complication in the transition to adoptive parenthood is the social stigma that is still attached to being an adoptive parent (Miall, 1987). Although often hearing comments about "what a wonderful thing they are doing," prospective adoptive parents also recognize that most individuals place a higher value on biological parenthood than adoptive parenthood. Moreover, when they hear others commenting that "it's too bad they couldn't have one of their own," these same parents are forced to recognize the "second-class status" of adoptive family connections in our society. In turn, this realization may lead them to begin to second-guess their decision to adopt as well as their ability to establish a loving, secure relationship with an adopted child.

Although the decision to adopt a child and the transition to adoptive parenthood is associated with considerable stress, prospective adoptive parents generally handle the challenges encountered quite well (Brodzinsky & Huffman, 1988). As they move through this period, individuals usually manifest a growing confidence in their emerging identity and role as adoptive parents. In fact, recent research comparing first-time adoptive parents-to-be and couples who were first-time biological parents-to-be has found no substantive differences in psychological adjustment and coping behavior between the groups (Levy-Shiff, Bar, & Har-Even, 1990).

INFANCY

The infant who is placed for adoption does not recognize or understand his or her unique family status. Consequently, from the child's perspective, there are no specific tasks associated with adoption that must be mastered during this period—only those life tasks that are similar to the ones experienced by most other young children. But for adoptive parents, the challenge of confronting and coping with specific adoption-related tasks continues.

With the arrival of the child, adoptive parents must begin to create a caregiving environment that not only will meet the more universal needs found among all children, but also those needs that are specific to their adopted child. First, and foremost, they must help their young child to become integrated into the family and develop a sense of safety, security, and trust that will become the foundation for healthy psychological development. Many adoptive parents worry that the process of establishing secure attachment bonds between the child and themselves will be more difficult because they did not carry the child in utero and were not present for the birth and perhaps the first days or weeks of the child's life. This worry is often heightened when earlier conflicts about infertility still exist (Brodzinsky, 1997) or when there has been ambivalent support from family and friends regarding the adoption. Yet research by Singer et al. (1985) suggests that when children are placed for adoption early in life—generally before six months of age—there is little, if any, difference in the quality of mother-infant attachment in adoptive and nonadoptive families. Attachment difficulties are more like to occur, however, when children are placed for adoption beyond this age period (Yarrow & Goodwin, 1973; Yarrow et al., 1973). These problems generally are thought to be the result of either neglect or abuse in the biological family, the cumulative disruptive effects of multiple foster care placements, or the damaging effects of early rearing in institutional and orphanage environments (Hughes, 1997). Parents must not only establish a caregiving environment that fosters strong and secure parent-child bonds, but also one that will be conducive to supporting a healthy exploration of adoption-related issues on the part of the child in the coming years. Parents need to develop realistic expectations about how adoption is likely to color the family's life. They must be willing to acknowledge, at least to a moderate extent, the differences that inherently are part of adoptive family life. At the heart of these differences is the recognition and acceptance that their children are inextricably bound to two families—the one in which they are living and the one they were born to. Adoptive parents must begin to explore their own feelings about the birth family in preparation for sharing with their children, in the coming years, information about their origins and the story of their adoption. They also must consider how they will handle the curiosity and questions of others in relation to their unique family status. This is especially true of couples who adopt across racial lines, where the obvious physical dissimilarities between parents and children preclude keeping the adoption a private family matter.

TODDLERHOOD AND
THE PRESCHOOL YEARS

With the emergence of language and representational thought on the part of the child, the adoptive family enters an extremely important period of the family life cycle. For the first time, parents can begin to engage their children in discussions about adoption. Although there is some controversy about the most appropriate time to tell children about their adoption (Brodzinsky, 1984; Brodzinsky et al., 1992; Wieder, 1977), most parents begin this process between 2 and 4 years of age. Thus, for parents, the primary adoption-related task of this period is sharing with children the reality of their adoption and the circumstances of their relinquishment.

Adoption revelation is inevitably experienced as anxiety arousing for parents. Whereas previously they were concerned almost exclusively with integrating the child into their family and consolidating family bonds, now they must begin a process of *family differentiation*. In other words, children must be told that although they are part of the family, they also are connected to another family—that they have a birth mother and birth father who are different from the parents who are raising them.

Adoptive parents often worry about how their children will assimilate this information and how it will affect their adjustment and family relationships. Some parents, fearing that their children may be traumatized by the information, procrastinate and delay telling them about their adoption. Moreover, when they begin sharing information with the child, these same parents do so very hesitantly, and often seek to "get through" the telling process as quickly as possible and avoid any probing questions on the child's part. In addition, these parents tend to minimize the differences between adoptive and nonadoptive family life. Unresolved infertility issues and difficulty in accepting the nonbiological connection to their child often lie at the heart of parents' heightened anxiety and ambivalence about the adoption revelation process (Brodzinsky, 1997).

In reality, most adoptive parents appear to cope with the telling process reasonably well, without undue anxiety, evasion, defensiveness, or distortion. These parents appear to have worked through most of their conflicts about infertility and the lack of a biological connection to their child and are able to recognize the normality of the child's uncertainty, confusion, and ambivalence in response to adoption information. As a result, they usually approach the telling process with greater self-confidence and security in the parent-child relationship.

If the task of adoptive parents is to tell children about their unique family status, it is the child's task to understand the information presented. Of course, this raises the question about what exactly the telling process accomplishes at this young age. To what extent does the preschool-age child comprehend the meaning of adoption, and what expectations do parents have in sharing this information with their children? Research by Brodzinsky and his colleagues indicates that although children in the preschool years usually are able to label themselves as being adopted and begin to learn their adoption story, there is relatively little understanding of what they are talking about (Brodzinsky et al., 1984, 1986). In a sense they are learning the language of adoption, but do not yet comprehend the implications of the information being discussed.

Interestingly, adoptive parents often overestimate what children understand about adoption at this time (Brodzinsky, 1983). Hearing a child identify himself as being adopted, and reporting that he has another mother and father, often leads parents to assume that the child has a fairly realistic, albeit simplistic, sense of his origins and current family status. Yet this is seldom the case. For children of this developmental period, adoption typically is but a self-label, associated with an interesting story shared by parents in the context of a warm, loving, and protective family environment. Thus, although young children may talk about being adopted, and often express quite positive feelings about this part of their life (Singer, Brodzinsky, & Braff, 1982), they have very little awareness of what adoption means. It is not until the middle childhood years, with the emergence of more sophisticated cognitive abilities and social sensitivities, that children begin to appreciate the profound implications of their unique family status.

MIDDLE CHILDHOOD

During the elementary school years, roughly from 6 to 12 years of age, a number of significant developmental achievements occur that set the stage for important changes in the way children view adoption as well as the type of adoption-related tasks that family members must manage. For children, this is a time of curiosity, exploration, and mastery of the world around them, including the world of adoption. With the emergence of new cognitive skills, especially those related to problem solving and logical reasoning, children develop a deeper understanding of their adoptive family status, which typically affects their emotional adjustment and family relationships (Brodzinsky, Schechter, Braff, & Singer, 1984; Brodzinsky, Singer, & Braff, 1984). Around 6 years of age, children begin by differentiating between adoption and birth as alternative ways of forming a family. They recognize that although all children enter the world the same way—by being born— family membership can result from either being born or adopted into the family. In addition, it is understood that being adopted means having birth parents who are independent of the individuals who are raising them. Over the next few years, children's sensitivity to, and appreciation of, the implications of being adopted grow quite rapidly. For example, as children develop the ability to conceptualize another's perspective, and reason about problem-solving options, they often begin to reevaluate the relinquishment decision by the birth mother in light of other possible options that might have been chosen by her. "If she was too poor to care for me," the child might ask, "why didn't she get a job?" "If she was alone and didn't have anyone to help care for a baby, why didn't she get married, or ask her parents for help?" "If she didn't know how to care for a baby, why didn't someone teach her?" These simple solutions for the complex problems confronting the birth parent represent the child's efforts to resolve the mystery and confusion surrounding the question of why the relinquishment happened in the first place.

Children's understanding of the family also complicates feelings about being adopted. Before 6 to 7 years of age, children generally define a family in terms of geographical and affectional criteria. Thus, whoever lives with or takes care of the child is likely to be thought of as part of the family. Appreciation of biological connection as a criterion for family membership typically is absent in the preschool and early elementary school years. As a result, the assurances offered by adoptive parents that they (parents and children) are all part of the family, and will be so forever, are usually well received and accepted by the young child. But around 7 to 8 years of age, children begin to recognize that families are usually defined in terms of biological connections (Newman, Roberts, & Syre, 1993). Realizing that they are not tied to their parents by birth, but do have birth parents elsewhere, many adopted children begin to express some confusion and anxiety during this time about their status as family members.

Another crucial achievement influencing children's adoption adjustment at this time is the development of logical reciprocity. Children now spontaneously recognize that to have been adopted, one first had to have been surrendered or relinquished by birth parents. This is a profound insight for adoptees. It forces them to examine adoption not only in terms of having gained a family, but as having *lost* one as well.

For the first time, especially for infant-placed children, adoption is appraised as involving loss (Nickman, 1985; Smith & Brodzinsky, 1994). With time, the sense of loss can become quite profound, although subtle and not always observable to the outsider. There is the loss of birth parents, birth siblings, and extended birth family; status loss associated with adoption-related stigma; loss of cultural, ethnic, and racial heritage; loss of genealogical connections; loss of stability within the adoptive family; and loss of identity. It is this experience of loss that is thought to be tied, at least by some adoption theorists, to the increased psychological problems among adopted children during middle childhood and adolescence (D. M. Brodzinsky, 1990; Nickman, 1985).

The many changes that children are going through regarding adoption during this period can be quite confusing and troubling for adoptive parents. As children struggle to understand the personal meaning of being adopted and cope with adoption-related loss, parents must recognize that the ambivalence about being adopted experienced by their child is perfectly normal. It represents neither a failure on their part nor an indication of psychopathology within the child. Rather, the growing ambivalence is part of a normal grief reaction that emerges when the adoptee begins to focus on the inherent loss associated with adoption (D. M. Brodzinsky, 1990).

The challenge for adoptive parents at this time is to create a caregiving environment that supports their youngster's growing curiosity about his or her origins, reinforces a positive view of the birth family, maintains open communication about adoption among family members, and supports the child's efforts to "work through" feelings about adoption-related loss. It is especially important for adoptive parents to guard against creating an impenetrable psychological barrier between the adoptive and biological family. To do so increases the risk that children will experience a sense of divided loyalty, making it difficult for them to share their thoughts and feelings about adoption as well as to integrate their adoption status into a healthy sense of self during the coming years.

ADOLESCENCE

The adolescent years are associated with a host of significant changes in physical, cognitive, emotional, and social functioning. Many of these developmental changes, in turn, are tied to new adjustment issues for adoptees and their parents. The most fundamental task for the adopted teenager is establishing a stable and secure sense of self. In part, this process involves becoming comfortable with the physical self. For some adoptees, the lack of physical similarity between themselves and their parents can be quite disconcerting. Unlike most of their peers, they cannot look into the faces of their parents and siblings and see reflections of themselves. This is especially true for individuals placed across racial lines.

Another aspect of physical development that poses some unique psychological issues for the adoptee is sexual maturation. As adopted teenagers experience sexual feelings and begin to experiment with sexual behavior, they often find themselves in a quandary regarding whom they wish to emulate—their adoptive parents, who typically urge restraint, or their birth parents, whose early sexual behavior may have led to their very existence. Sometimes adoptees view sex as a symbolic means of undoing the adoption. Adopted adolescent females, in particular, may fantasize about getting pregnant and nurturing their infant in a way their birth parent could not or would not do for them. Carrie, a 16-year-old girl seen in psychotherapy by one of us, once remarked,

> My birth mom had me when she was 16. If she could have sex at 16, why can't I? . . . Sometimes I think about getting pregnant. If I do, though, I would keep my baby, and care for it, and love it, and never give it away, the way I was.

Many adoption theorists have emphasized that the ability to establish a stable and secure ego identity is more complex for adoptees because they have been cut off from their origins and often are prevented from gaining information about their birth heritage (Brodzinsky et al., 1992; Hoopes, 1990). Sorosky et al. (1975), in particular, have emphasized four fundamental issues that complicate identity development in the adoptee:

1. problems in early object relations that impede the emergence of trust and security in the infancy years;
2. difficulties in resolving Oedipal feelings toward adoptive family members with whom one is unrelated biologically;
3. the tendency of adoptees, in response to conflict, to overuse the splitting defense, in which one set of parents (either adoptive or biological) is seen as "all good" and the other as "all bad"; and
4. confusion and uncertainty regarding genealogical continuity that is tied to limited knowledge about one's ancestors.

It is during the adolescent years that many adoptees begin to think more seriously about searching for additional information about their origins and eventually making contact with birth relatives. Quite often there is a great deal of ambivalence about the search process. On the one hand, adoptees want to know about their birth parents and the circumstances of the relinquishment, yet they often are afraid of what they will find out. In addition, they may worry about the adoptive parents' reactions to their interest in searching. Will their parents support them or be upset and view searching as a sign of disloyalty? For the most part, searching during the adolescent years is restricted to gathering information about one's birth parents and extended birth family, perhaps visiting one's birthplace, and for some youngsters, exploring their cultural, ethnic, or racial heritage. Attempting to make contact with birth family members usually is not an activity that most adolescents engage in. Rather, this type of search generally begins in the late 20s or early 30s (Schechter & Bertocci, 1990).

As their adolescent children take on the challenges of integrating adoption into their emerging sense of themselves, adoptive parents have their own unique adoption-related tasks to consider. First, they must continue to foster a child-rearing environment that is conducive to open and honest communication about adoption issues. Second, they must continue to help their youngsters cope with adoption-related loss and support the grief work that naturally follows the experience of loss. Third, they must recognize that the search for origins, which began earlier in the form of questions about the birth family, is likely to continue in a more complex way, leading their adolescent children to want more information and perhaps even contact with birth family members. Adoptive parents must be able to validate and normalize their teenagers' interest in searching and work with them to develop realistic, age-appropriate plans that meet their youngsters' needs, but also inform them about possibilities that they cannot yet envision. Finally, adoptive parents must not only acknowledge their children's dual connection to two families, but also find ways of valuing *both* connections. For the teenager who is struggling to understand the meaning of being adopted, and integrating this aspect of his life into a healthy sense of self, feedback from parents that reflects a highly negative view of the birth family not only is likely to undermine a secure ego identity, but create conflicted relationships within the adoptive family as well.

SUMMARY

For parents, adjustment to adoption begins with their struggle with infertility and the consideration of adoption as a means of achieving parenthood. It continues throughout the early family life cycle years as they integrate their children into the family and begin a process of sharing adoption information with them. Once children know they are adopted, they too will begin an adjustment process that involves integrating the meaning of their unique family status and their dual connection to two families into an emerging sense of self. For both parents and children, the adjustment to adoption will be a lifelong process, with new tasks and challenges emerging at each stage of the family life cycle, not only through adolescence, as outlined in this chapter, but into adulthood as well (Brodzinsky et al., 1992). How children and their parents handle these unique tasks and challenges will vary considerably. Although most adoptees will develop in very normal ways and show little evidence of emotional or behavioral problems, others will have significant psychological difficulties and require professional intervention.

4

INFANT-PLACED ADOPTED CHILDREN

Modern adoption practice emerged in response to a pressing societal need for improved care for dependent and orphaned children. Research had demonstrated quite clearly that children raised in orphanages and other large group care facilities suffered significant developmental delays in many areas of psychological functioning (Goldfarb, 1945; Spitz, 1945). The development of family foster care, although an improvement over institutional life, also was shown to be associated with significant negative consequences for children, particularly those who lingered in care for long periods or who experienced multiple placements (Bohman, 1970; Fanshel & Shinn, 1978). Adoption, in contrast, was viewed by child welfare professionals as providing a permanent and nurturing family environment in which children could grow and flourish. Because of the long tradition of viewing adoption as a solution for the problems of children needing permanent homes, professionals and the lay public had difficulty in accepting the notion that the solution, itself, could, at times, be a problem. It was not until the early work of Kirk (1964) and Schechter and his colleagues (Schechter, 1960; Schechter et al., 1964) that any systematic attention was paid to the question of psychological risk associated with adoption. In the past three decades, a rich body of empirical and clinical work has emerged on this issue. In the present chapter we will focus primarily on psychological outcomes for children placed as infants in same-race families and in traditional closed adoptions. Chapters 5 through 7 will cover psychological outcomes of special needs adopted children, interracially adopted children, and children in open adoptions, respectively.

ASSESSING PSYCHOLOGICAL RISK
ASSOCIATED WITH ADOPTION

The question of how infant-placed adopted children and their families fare psychologically has been examined primarily from three perspectives:

1. the percentage of adoptees in various types of mental health settings,
2. the nature of presenting symptomatology in adopted children seen in clinical settings, and
3. the behavioral and personality characteristics and adjustment patterns of adopted children from community-based samples.

A fourth area of research on rates and correlates of adoption disruption—the removal of a child from an adoptive home prior to legal finalization—has focused primarily on special needs placements and consequently will be discussed in the next chapter.

Percentage of Adoptees in Mental Health Settings

One of the first ways in which researchers sought to gather information on psychological risk in adoption was to examine the percentage of adoptees in outpatient and inpatient mental health facilities. To address this question, however, one first must know the baseline for adoption in the general population of children. Unfortunately, national adoption statistics in the United States are difficult to come by because the federal government no longer systematically collects these types of data (Stolley, 1993). However, recent estimates, including one large-scale national health survey (Zill, 1985), indicate that approximately 2% of the population of children are being raised by adoptive parents with whom they have no biological connection.

Research has consistently shown that adopted children are overrepresented in both outpatient and inpatient mental health settings (Wierzbicki, 1993). Individual studies from the United States, Canada, and Great Britain suggest that the proportion of adopted children in outpatient clinical settings is between 3% and 13% (Brinich & Brinich, 1982; Goldberg & Wolkind, 1992; Kotsopoulos et al., 1988; Schechter, 1960; Simon & Senturia, 1966; Work & Anderson, 1971), with a conservative mid-range estimate of 4% to 5%—at least twice what one would expect given their representation in the general population. Record review research on inpatient mental health populations indicates an even greater percentage of adoptees in these facilities—between 9% and 21% (Dickson, Heffron, & Parker, 1990; Kim et al., 1988; Piersma,

1987; Rogeness et al., 1988; Work and Anderson, 1971). The latter figures suggest that adoptees appear to be at least five to eight times as likely to be referred to an inpatient mental health facility compared with their nonadopted counterparts.

Although overrepresentation in outpatient and inpatient mental health centers usually has been interpreted as suggesting that infant-placed adopted children are at increased psychological risk compared with nonadopted children, alternative explanations are also possible. Adoptive parents may be more likely to refer their children to a mental health professional than nonadoptive parents, either because of their own anxiety and insecurity (Brodzinsky, 1997; Hartman & Laird, 1990) or because of greater vigilance regarding potential psychological problems in their children resulting from working with social service and mental health professionals during the preplacement period. A recent study by Warren (1992) found some support for a referral bias among adoptive parents. In reanalyzing data from a 1981 national health survey of 3,698 adolescents, Warren found that, although adopted teenagers from 12 to 17 years of age were more likely to manifest behavior problems than nonadopted youth, they also were more likely to be referred for mental health services by their parents even when displaying relatively few or minor symptoms.

Another possible explanation for the increased rate of adoptees in mental health settings is that the professionals involved may have a more negative view of adopted children—that is, they may attribute greater problems to adoptees compared with nonadoptees, even for the same behaviors and symptoms. Research has produced mixed results regarding this issue. Weiss (1987) found little difference in the way mental health professionals responded to hypothetical descriptions of adopted versus nonadopted adolescents. Kojis (1990), on the other hand, found that psychologists gave more serious diagnoses and recommended more intensive treatment plans when responding to hypothetical vignettes describing the behavior and symptoms of adopted adolescents compared with nonadopted youth. Thus, although adopted children and adolescents appear to be overrepresented in both outpatient and inpatient mental health facilities, at least part of the reason for this finding may be a referral and response bias on the part of adoptive parents and professionals.

Clinical Symptomatology in Adopted Children

A second area of research interest has been on the type of symptoms typically manifested by adopted children in clinical and special education settings. At issue here is whether adoptees are more likely than nonadoptees to manifest specific types of adjustment problems. The results have been inconsistent.

Some research has found increased rates of academic problems and learning disabilities among adopted children (Silver, 1970, 1989). In a recent statewide survey of public and private school special education programs in New Jersey, Brodzinsky and Steiger (1991) reported that adopted children accounted for nearly 7% of the children classified for educational purposes as neurologically impaired, 5% of the children classified as perceptually impaired, and 7% of the children classified as emotionally disturbed. These figures are significantly higher than what one would expect given the rate of adoption in the general population. In contrast, Wadsworth, DeFries, and Fulker (1993) found little or no evidence of increased risk for learning problems in infant-placed adoptees.

Other research has reported that adoptees are overrepresented among those youngsters diagnosed with attention deficit hyperactivity disorder (Deutsch et al., 1982; Dickson et al., 1990) as well as those children and teenagers who are characterized by conduct disorder and related disruptive behavior (Fullerton, Goodrich, & Berman, 1986; Kotsopoulos et al., 1988; Kotsopoulos, Walker, Copping, Cote, & Stavrakaki, 1993; Menlove, 1965; Schechter et al., 1964; Weiss, 1985). Goldberg and Wolkind (1992), on the other hand, found increased conduct problems only among adopted girls compared with nonadopted girls; no differences were noted for boys. In addition, three other studies reported no differences in conduct problems between adopted and nonadopted youth seen in clinical settings (Dickson et al., 1990; Piersma, 1987; Rogeness et al., 1988).

In some studies, adoptees in clinical settings also have been found to manifest higher rates of substance abuse (Holden, 1991; Marshall, Marshall, & Heer, 1994), eating disorders (Holden, 1991), and personality disorder (Rogeness et al., 1988; Schechter et al., 1964; Simon & Senturia, 1966) compared with their nonadopted peers. Weiss (1985), however, failed to confirm higher rates of personality disorder and substance abuse in adoptees. In addition, there appears to be little difference between clinical samples of adopted and nonadopted children for internalizing symptomatology such as anxiety disorder and depression (Kotsopoulos et al., 1988, 1993; Rogeness et al., 1988) or for psychosis (Goldberg & Wolkind, 1992; Piersma, 1988; Rogeness et al., 1988).

Finally, adopted and nonadopted youth also have been distinguished in terms of various characteristics related to psychiatric hospitalization. For example, research suggests that adoptees are younger at first admission to a psychiatric facility and are more likely to have had a previous hospitalization for mental health problems (Dickson et al., 1990; Weiss, 1985). Adopted youth also are more likely to have longer stays in the psychiatric hospital (Dickson et al., 1990) and to run away from the inpatient facility (Fullerton et al., 1986).

In summary, although some support has been found for increased risk for learning problems and externalizing behavior (e.g., hyperactivity, aggression, oppositionalism, substance abuse) among adopted children and youth, the results are not consistent across studies, perhaps because of sampling and methodological differences.

Psychological Characteristics of Adopted Children in Community Settings

Because of the limitations in generalizing from clinical studies, a growing number of researchers have examined psychological and behavioral characteristics, and patterns of development, in adopted and nonadopted children from community-based samples. Although most of these studies are cross-sectional in design, several important longitudinal investigations also have been reported.

Cross-Sectional Studies. There have been few, if any, significant differences reported between adopted and nonadopted infants, toddlers, and pre-schoolers. For example, Singer et al. (1985) found no differences in adoptive and nonadoptive mother-infant dyads in quality of attachment at 14 months of age using the Strange Situation paradigm. Similarly, no group differences have been found for infant temperament (Carey, Lipton, & Myers, 1974), mental and motor functioning (Plomin & DeFries, 1985) and communication development (Thompson & Plomin, 1988).

Some studies with older subjects also have failed to find differences between adopted and nonadopted children in terms of adjustment problems or patterns of behavioral and personality characteristics (Mikawa & Boston, 1968; Norvell & Guy, 1977; Stein & Hoopes, 1985). In addition, a recent multistate study by the Search Institute on 881 adolescents, adopted in infancy, generally found them to be doing quite well. Few differences were observed in these youngsters in identity, family relations, and mental health compared with their nonadopted siblings (Benson, Sharma, & Roehlkepartain, 1994). Moreover, when assessed against a public school comparison group on well-being and high-risk behavior indexes, adopted youth were actually shown to fare better.

In contrast to the studies above, other research on community-based samples supports the position that, beginning around 6 to 7 years of age, adopted children are more likely than their nonadopted peers to show increased adjustment problems. Lindholm and Touliatos (1980), for example, reported that teachers rated adopted children, from kindergarten through eighth grade, as having a higher incidence than nonadopted children of conduct problems, personality problems, and socialized delinquency, but not immaturity or psychosis. Several studies by Brodzinsky and his colleagues also have found increased adjustment problems for adopted school-age children. The first study (Brodzinsky et al., 1984) compared 130 adopted children, 6 to 11 years of age, with a matched sample of nonadopted children on parent (Child Behavior Checklist, CBCL) and teacher (Hahnemann Elementary School Behavior Rating Scale) ratings of adjustment. Results indicated that adoptive parents rated their children as lower in social competence and higher in behavior problems than did nonadoptive parents. Specifically, adopted girls were rater lower in social interaction and school success as well as higher in internalizing problems, especially depression and social withdrawal, and externalizing problems, especially hyperactive behavior, delinquency, aggression, and cruelty. Adopted boys were rated lower in school success than nonadoptees as well as higher in uncommunicative behavior and externalizing problems, such as hyperactivity, aggression, and delinquency. In addition, teacher ratings consistently showed adoptees to be manifesting poorer adjustment across a wide range of school-related behavior and achievement than their nonadopted peers. Moreover, in a reanalysis of the previous data, Brodzinsky et al. (1987) found that adopted children were rated by parents as more likely to fall within the clinical range (T score > 70) on at least one CBCL scale compared with nonadopted children (36% versus 14%). In a third study, examining the impact of parental divorce on adopted and nonadopted children, Brodzinsky, Hitt, and Smith (1993) noted that adopted boys were rated by their parents as higher in uncommunicative behavior and externalizing symptoms such as hyperactivity and aggression than nonadopted boys; no differences were found for girls as a function of adoption status.

Using data from a cohort of 1,265 children born in 1977 in Christchurch, New Zealand, Fergusson, Lynskey, and Horwood (1995) compared the psychological adjustment among three groups of children when they were 16 years old: children raised by two biological parents (842 subjects), children born to single mothers who subsequently were placed for adoption in infancy (32 subjects), and children who were raised by their single mothers (60 subjects). Generally speaking, children raised by single mothers showed more problems than individuals from the other two groups. On the other hand, adopted adolescents manifested a higher incidence of externalizing problems than nonadopted youth living in two-parent families, especially in conduct and oppositional disorders, attention deficit hyperactivity disorder, and use of cigarettes and marijuana. No differences were noted for alcohol use and involvement with the police. Furthermore, no differences were found between adoptees and nonadoptees from two-parent families for internalizing problems such as anxiety, depression, suicidal behavior, and self-esteem. Reporting on data from a national health survey, Zill (1985) noted that at 12 to 17 years of age, adopted teenagers were rated higher by their parents on a behavior problem index and lower in school achievement than nonadopted youth. In addition, adoptees were 2.5 times more likely than nonadoptees to have ever seen a mental health professional and more than three times more likely to have received such help within the past year. Another large-scale health survey (Lipman, Offord, Racine, & Boyle, 1992), this time from Canada, reported that adopted boys, 4 to 16 years of age, had a higher frequency of psychiatric disorder and school problems than nonadopted boys, whereas adopted girls had a higher use of licit and illicit substances than nonadopted girls. The group differences for the boys disappeared, however, when various demographic factors (e.g., child's and parent's age, medical problems) were controlled statistically. Finally, a third large-scale, multistate study, using children's self-report data, also explored adjustment differences in adopted and nonadopted children (Sharma, McGue, & Benson, 1996a). A sample of 4,682 adopted children, from grades 6 to 12, matched to an equal number of nonadopted youth, responded to a self-report instrument measuring 12 factors associated with various individual adjustment and family functioning variables. Results indicated that adoptees reported significantly higher rates of licit drug use, illicit drug use, negative emotionality, and antisocial behavior. They also rated themselves as lower in optimism/self-confidence and school adjustment and rated their parents as lower in nurturance and involvement but not in parental control. Despite the consistent pattern suggesting more maladjustment among adopted children and teenagers, the researchers noted that the magnitude of difference between the groups in most outcome areas was actually quite small, with an effect size never exceeding .26.

Longitudinal Studies. Four longitudinal investigations from three different countries have examined adjustment differences between adopted and nonadopted children at various points in development. Several studies have used a cohort sample born in Great Britain in a single week in March 1958.

When the children were seven years old, Seglow, Pringle, and Wedge (1972) compared 180 adopted children with two other groups: children born within a marriage and raised by their parents and children born outside of marriage and raised by their birth mother. Teacher ratings of general adjustment indicated that the children raised by their birth mother outside of marriage were significantly less well adjusted than both the adopted children and those children raised within a marriage. In addition, although no overall difference in adjustment was found between the latter two groups, when the data were divided by gender, adopted boys were rated as more maladjusted than nonadopted boys but no group differences were found for girls. When these same children were 11 years old, Lambert and Streather (1980) once again obtained teacher ratings of children's adjustment. This time both adopted boys and girls were found to manifest more maladjustment than the two groups of nonadopted children. In addition, the overall adjustment of adoptees appeared to have deteriorated between 7 and 11 years of age. New data were collected on this cohort when the subjects were 16 and 23 years old (Maughan & Pickles, 1990). At 16 years of age, teacher ratings indicated that children born outside of marriage and raised by their birth mother were significantly less well adjusted than the adolescent group born within a marriage and raised by their birth parents. Adopted teenagers, on the other hand, fell in between these two groups but were not different from either of them—an exception being in the area of peer relationships, in which adoptees were reported to have more problems compared with nonadopted children. Finally, at 23 years of age, the researchers employed the Malaise Inventory as a measure of emotional disturbance and found no differences between adopted youth and the group of young adults who were born within a marriage and raised by their parents, with an exception of more job instability among adopted males. In summary, the results from the longitudinal study of this cohort suggest that adjustment difficulties for adoptees that emerge in middle childhood and the early teenage years are largely gone by late adolescence to young adulthood.

A prospective adoption study in Sweden also followed a cohort of individuals from the 1950s who were originally registered for adoption by their birth mothers. Of the total sample, 164 were eventually placed for adoption (Group 1); for 213 of these youngsters, the birth mother changed her mind and raised the child (Group 2); the remaining 124 children were not adopted and lived in long-term foster care (Group 3). Bohman and his colleagues (Bohman, 1970, 1990; Bohman & Sigvardsson, 1978, 1979, 1980) reported outcome data on these groups compared with community comparison groups at four developmental points: 11 years, 15 years, 18 years, and 23 years. At

11 years of age, adopted boys, but not girls, were rated by teachers as having a higher rate of nervous and behavioral disturbances compared with a group of classmate controls. Similar findings, but of greater magnitude, were found in the comparisons between Groups 2 and 3 and their classmate controls. When the children were 15 years old, teacher ratings were once again collected on various aspects of school, social, and emotional adjustment and compared with ratings of classmate controls. Although adopted youngsters still tended to have lower school grades and adjustment scores, comparisons with the control group were only occasionally significant. As Bohman (1990) noted, "The relatively high rate of maladjustment found in Group 1 at age 11 now seemed to have been compensated" (p. 100). In contrast, clear evidence of deterioration in both social and school adjustment between the ages of 11 and 15 years for Group 2 (children living with their birth mother) and Group 3 (children living in long-term foster care), compared with classmate controls, was observed. At 18 years of age, data were collected from the military records of male subjects in areas related to physical, psychological, and social adjustment. No differences were found in patterns of adjustment between adoptees and controls selected from the general population. On the other hand, males from Groups 2 and 3 continued to manifest poorer psychological adjustment compared with controls. Finally, when subjects were 23 years old, researchers gathered data from public records of criminal behavior and alcohol abuse. No differences were found in the incidence of criminality and alcohol abuse between adopted males or females and their nonadopted controls. A similar pattern was found for individuals growing up with their birth mother. In contrast, males, but not females, growing up in foster care were significantly more likely to be registered for criminal behavior, alcohol abuse, or both compared with control subjects. This study, like the British study noted above, suggests that although adoption may place a youngster at risk for adjustment problems in childhood, by middle adolescence, and certainly by young adulthood, the problems are greatly diminished, if not eliminated.

Longitudinal data from the Delaware Family Study also shed light on developmental patterns in adopted children's adjustment (Hoopes, 1982; Stein & Hoopes, 1985). At 5 years of age, adopted children were rated by researchers, but not by parents, as more fearful, less confident, and less task-motivated than nonadopted children. Problems in adjustment among adoptees, as measured by children's self-reports and teacher reports, but not parent reports, became even more apparent during middle childhood. When the teenagers were between 15 and 18 years, however, no differences between adoptees and nonadoptees were found for identity development and self-image.

Finally, the Colorado Adoption Project also has contributed longitudinal data on the relative adjustment of adopted and nonadopted children. Data collected during infancy and the toddler years indicate no differences between adopted and nonadopted children in terms of mental or motor functioning, communication ability, and home environment (Plomin & DeFries, 1985; Thompson & Plomin, 1988). Between 4 and 7 years old, however, adopted boys were more likely to be classified by researchers as at risk for conduct problems (Coon, Carey, Corley, & Fulker, 1992). When the children were in first grade, adoptees performed more poorly in areas of reading and mathematics achievement than nonadopted children, although the difference between the groups was not great (Coon, Carey, Fulker, & DeFries, 1993). In addition, at 7 years of age, maternal ratings of externalizing behavior, aggression, and attention problems, and teacher ratings of externalizing behavior, aggression, delinquency, attention problems, social problems, and thought problems were greater for adopted than nonadopted children, although once again, adoption status accounted for a relatively small proportion of the total variance (Braungart-Rieker, Rende, Plomin, DeFries, & Fulker, 1995). Finally, Wadsworth et al. (1993) assessed children's intellectual functioning, achievement test scores, and school placement at 7 and 12 years of age. Results indicated that at both ages, verbal IQ was significantly lower for adopted compared with nonadopted children, although the mean group difference accounted for only about 2% to 4% of the variance. No group differences were found in achievement test scores or in the proportion of adopted and nonadopted children in special education classes.

Psychological Risk in Adoption: Summary and Critique

Whether adopted children are seen as at risk psychologically depends on the body of research that is examined. Epidemiological studies focusing on the percentage of adoptees in outpatient and inpatient mental health settings clearly support the position that adoption is associated with psychological risk. Research on presenting symptomatology, on the other hand, suggests that although adoptees seen in clinical settings may be more prone to display externalizing behaviors and academic difficulties than nonadoptees, they clearly manifest a wide range of behaviors and are probably more similar than different from their nonadopted counterparts. Finally, research focusing on community-based samples suggests that adjustment differences between adopted and nonadopted individuals, when they exist, are more likely to be found in middle childhood and early adolescence than at other developmental periods. Furthermore, even when significant group differences are present, they often are relatively small (cf. Braungart-Rieker et al., 1995; Sharma et al., 1996a). In fact, virtually all the studies reported suggest that the majority of adoptees are well within the normal range of functioning. Consequently, care must be taken not to overinterpret or overgeneralize the findings from this body of research (Brodzinsky, 1993; Haugaard, in press). It may well be that the group differences between adopted and nonadopted children are accounted for by a small percentage of adoptees whose adjustment is much more deviant than the majority of the sample. Haugaard (in press) suggests this could be detected by examining group differences in the standard deviation and distribution of the adjustment scores.

Another problem in interpreting the results of adoption outcome research is the influence of methodological difficulties that have plagued the field (Brodzinsky, 1993). In the past, most research utilized clinical samples, which limited the generalizability of the findings. Small sample sizes have also been a problem until fairly recently. Like most areas of human research, the use of volunteers in adoption studies raises questions about the representativeness of the subject samples and the generalizability of the data to the broader population of adoptees and their families. Studies that recruit adoptees from limited sources (e.g., a single agency) also run the risk of sampling biases. In addition, some studies have combined children placed as infants and those placed in later years. Later-placed children, however, often experience early neglect, abuse, and foster care, which are associated with poorer adjustment outcomes and can magnify mean group differences. The use of inadequately validated adjustment measures and the failure to employ comparison groups has also made it difficult to interpret the results of some studies. Furthermore, there is even a question as to which comparison group is most appropriate to use in adoption research. For example, should one use a comparison group of children who come from the socioeconomic background of the biological family, or a group being raised in families similar to the adoptive families? Should groups of children in foster homes and residential facilities be employed? Researchers who compare adoptees with children living in families from comparable socioeconomic environments often find them to be at risk psychologically (Brodzinsky et al., 1984; Brodzinsky et al., 1987). On the other hand, when adopted children are compared with agemates who are living in families similar to the socioeconomic environment of the birth family, or who are in foster care or residential facilities, they very often are shown to fare significantly better than these other groups (Bohman, 1970, 1990; Fergusson et al., 1995; Maughan & Pickles, 1990; Seglow et al., 1972). The latter finding has been used to support the notion—and rightly so—that adoption protects children from the adverse effects of growing up in depriving and damaging environments. Finally, most adoption researchers have utilized cross-sectional designs, which severely limit the ability to understand developmental patterns in adoption adjustment. Fortunately, a number of prospective, longitudinal studies on adoption have been conducted. Of course, longitudinal designs have their own set of problems, perhaps the most significant being subject attrition. Researchers have long known that there is often a "selective dropout" in longitudinal designs, with those subjects who remain in the study being more motivated and better adjusted than those individuals who discontinue their involvement in the research. Selective-subject attrition can significantly distort the findings of follow-up research in longitudinal designs. Unfortunately, this problem often has not been addressed in longitudinal adoption research (e.g., Stein & Hoopes, 1985).

INDIVIDUAL DIFFERENCES IN ADOPTION ADJUSTMENT

Although adopted children may show a small, but significant, increase in adjustment problems compared with their nonadopted peers, there clearly is substantial variability in patterns of behavior and development among these youngsters, with most falling well within the normal range of functioning. Unfortunately, there has been relatively little research to date on correlates and predictors of adoption adjustment, especially for those children placed as infants. Consequently, we still have a poor understanding of why some adopted children do well, whereas others manifest seriously disturbed behavior and deviant family relationships. In this section, we examine some of the factors assumed to be related to individual differences in adoption outcome.

Genetic and Prenatal Influences in Adoption Adjustment

The significance of genetics in the development of such human characteristics as temperament, intelligence, personality, and sociability, as well as various personality disorders and major clinical syndromes, is now well established (Cadoret, 1990). In relation to the question of variability in adoption adjustment, the data have been extremely consistent in showing that adopted children and adults are more similar to their birth parents than their adoptive parents or nonbiological siblings in intelligence, interests, personality, and psychopathology (Cadoret, 1990). Furthermore, research has shown that increased risk for some of the more common problems seen in clinical samples of adoptees, such as hyperactivity, attention deficit disorder, substance abuse, and conduct disorders, occurs when adoptees are born to individuals with antisocial and alcoholic backgrounds (Cadoret & Gath, 1980; Cadoret et al., 1986).

Children's adoption adjustment also is thought to be influenced by a variety of adverse prenatal experiences, such as heightened maternal stress, poor maternal nutrition, inadequate medical care, and exposure to a host of teratogenic agents such as alcohol, drugs, and sexually transmitted diseases. These types of prenatal complications are known to increase the risk for postnatal developmental problems (Kopp, 1983) and have been found to be implicated in some of the adjustment difficulties of adoptees (Bohman, 1970; Everett & Schechter, 1971).

In short, understanding variability in adoption adjustment must begin with an appreciation of the biological foundation of development. Although certainly adoptees are significantly influenced by the adoptive family environment, much of the variability in their cognitive functioning, school success, personality, and psychological adjustment is likely to stem from the genetic endowment passed on by the biological parents and the quality of the prenatal environment offered by the biological mother.

Preplacement History

Although many children are placed for adoption immediately after birth, others enter their families later in childhood. Age at placement has been found to be one of the most powerful demographic predictors of placement stability and adoption adjustment. The older the child at the time of placement, the greater the risk that the placement will disrupt (Barth & Berry, 1988; Rosenthal, 1993). In a multi-state sample of 4,682 adopted children from grades 6 through 12, Sharma, McGue, and Benson (1996b) found greater adjustment difficulties among children placed at older ages compared with those placed in the early years of life. In addition, these researchers reported that the most serious adjustment problems, especially in areas related to licit drug use, illicit drug use, and antisocial behavior, were found in youngsters placed for adoption after 10 years of age.

Age at placement, however, is primarily a marker for early life experiences, many of which can be quite disruptive to children. Research indicates that children who experience multiple changes in caregiving environments as well as neglect or abuse, before being placed in an adoptive home, are at increased risk for developing adjustment problems (Barth & Berry, 1988; McRoy et al., 1988; Verhulst, Althaus, & Versluis-den Bieman, 1992). In fact, Verhulst et al. reported that age at placement did not contribute to the prediction of later maladjustment in an adolescent sample of international adoptees independent of these early disruptive life experiences.

Age Differences in Adoption Adjustment

As noted previously, no adjustment differences have been found between infant-placed adopted children and their nonadopted counterparts in infancy, toddlerhood, and the preschool years. However, beginning in middle child-hood—around 5 to 7 years of age—a number of studies have documented increased academic, psychological, and behavioral problems for adopted children, which appears to continue into early adolescence (Brodzinsky, 1993). This trend parallels the growing sense of ambivalence experienced by children during the childhood years regarding being adopted (Smith & Brodzinsky, 1994). Although the clinical literature (Sorosky et al., 1975) has often suggested that adolescence is a particularly vulnerable period for adoptees, research data, especially from longitudinal studies employing community samples (Bohman, 1990; Maughan & Pickles, 1990; Stein & Hoopes, 1985), do not support this position. As noted previously, the earlier adjustment problems observed in adopted children often disappear in middle and late adolescence. Whether this finding reflects a recovery or compensa-tion on the part of adopted children as they move through adolescence toward adulthood or the impact of methodological bias associated with selective dropout is not fully answerable at this time. Suffice it to state that currently neither cross-sectional nor longitudinal community-based research clearly supports the position that older adolescent adoptees are at greater risk for psychological problems than their nonadopted peers (see Verhulst & Versluis-den Bieman, 1995 for an exception to this conclusion).

Cognitive and Personality
Correlates of Adoption Adjustment

Brodzinsky (1987, 1990, 1993) has argued that developmental changes in children's adjustment to adoption are tied, in part, to their growing awareness of the meaning and implications of being adopted. As children enter the elementary school years, newly developed problem-solving skills and the emergence of logical thought are believed to set the stage for a more profound understanding of adoption, which in turn is thought to create a greater sense of ambivalence about being adopted. This is a time when children are often viewed by their parents as having some difficulty adjusting to their adoptive family status (Brodzinsky et al., 1986).

Children's appraisal of adoption-related loss and the coping efforts they use to manage such loss also are related to patterns of adoption adjustment, at least in middle childhood. Smith and Brodzinsky (1997) found that children who reported greater levels of negative affect about birth parent loss had higher levels of depression and lower self-worth. In addition, children who reported greater curiosity about their birth parents were rated by adoptive parents as higher in externalizing behavior problems. Children's coping strategies in response to adoption-related stress also were related to adjustment outcome. Those youngsters who more often coped with adoption issues through behavioral avoidant strategies reported greater anxiety and were rated by parents as having more behavior problems. In contrast, children who used problem-focused coping strategies in response to adoption-related stress were rated higher by parents on social competence.

Family Structure and Dynamics
in Adoption Adjustment

Although much has been written about the structure and dynamics of adoptive family life (Hajal & Rosenberg, 1991; Kirk, 1964; Reitz & Watson, 1992), relatively little empirical research has related family variables to children's adoption adjustment. Some researchers have examined variability in children's adjustment as a function of family structure or the child's ordinal position (Barth & Brooks, 1997; Brodzinsky & Brodzinsky, 1992; Brodzinsky et al., 1986; Kraus, 1978) with no consistent pattern emerging. In summarizing the research in this area, Brodzinsky and Brodzinsky (1992) concluded that "the order of adoption and the presence of biological children in the adoptive family, while complicating family dynamics, generally pose no serious impediments to successful adoption adjustment." Quality of attachment between parents and children has also been examined in relation to children's psychological adjustment. Using a parent Q-sort measure, Huffman and Brodzinsky (1997) found that children's security of attachment was the strongest predictor of psychological adjustment for both intraracial and interracial 4-year-old adopted children.

Beginning with the work of Kirk (1964), researchers have been concerned with the way adoptive family members communicate with one another about adoption. Kirk suggested that an open, "acknowledgment-of-difference" style of communication was more conducive to positive adjustment among family members than a closed, "rejection-of-difference" style. In support of this position, Stein and Hoopes (1985) reported that families with an open communication style had adolescents with fewer identity problems. Kaye (1990), on the other hand, found that families characterized by high levels of distinguishing between adoptive and biological relationships had adolescents with lower self-esteem and greater family problems. Brodzinsky (1993) has noted, however, that the latter finding is consistent with the idea that extreme styles at either end of the communication continuum—denial-of-difference at one end and insistence-of-difference at the other end—are less likely to facilitate healthy patterns of adoption adjustment.

Finally, a number of parenting dimensions, such as expectations, care-giving style, and parental emotional adjustment have been examined in relation to adoption outcome. In general, the research suggests that a warm and accepting attitude toward the child, coupled with realistic parenting expectations and satisfaction with adoptive parenthood, is associated with more positive adoption adjustment (Kadushin, 1980). In addition, adopted children have been shown to have fewer problems when adoptive parents are free of emotional problems and/or when there is no history of death or divorce within the adoptive family (Brodzinsky et al., 1993; Cadoret, 1990; Cadoret et al., 1985)

SUMMARY

For more than 30 years, mental health professionals have been exploring the question of psychological risk associated with adoption. With regard to infant-placed adoptees, the data appear somewhat inconsistent. Although epidemiological studies clearly point to an overrepresentation of adopted individuals in outpatient and inpatient mental health facilities, interpretation of this finding is complicated by the possibility of referral bias on the part of adoptive parents and response bias on the part of the professional community. In addition, whereas a majority of clinical studies show an increase in externalizing symptoms and academic difficulties in adoptees compared with nonadoptees, community-based studies fail to show a consistent pattern of group differences in behavior and adjustment. In most cases, differences between these groups tend to be found in middle childhood and early adolescence rather than at other developmental periods. Furthermore, even when group differences are observed, they generally are not large in magnitude. Thus, we must reiterate the caution raised by Brodzinsky et al. (1984) and Haugaard (in press) against overinterpreting the differences often found between adopted children and their nonadopted peers. These small, but significant, differences must not overshadow the fact that the vast majority of infant-placed adoptees do quite well and are within the normal range of psychological functioning. Future researchers would be well advised to spend less time focusing on the question of relative risk in adoption and more time examining those factors that influence the variability in adoption adjustment.

5

SPECIAL NEEDS ADOPTED CHILDREN

As we have noted previously, adoption policy and practice in the United States underwent significant change beginning in the late 1970s. Prior to this time, most adoptions involved the placement of healthy white infants in white families. However, a number of factors, including increased access to legal abortion services, greater societal acceptance of single parenthood, and better contraception methods, all led to a decrease in the availability of infants for adoption (Stolley, 1993). Coincidentally, the decline in adoptable babies occurred at the same time as an increase in public interest in adoption, as growing numbers of families delayed parenthood and began experiencing fertility problems. Thus, the parameters of adoption began to expand, as individuals and couples that previously would have adopted infants began considering the adoption of older children or children with physical, mental, or emotional problems (Rosenthal & Groze, 1992).

Over the same period, the growing awareness of child maltreatment, coupled with increasing rates of parental drug use, resulted in a dramatic increase in the number of children entering foster care (Gershenson, 1984), with rates rising by more than 50% between 1970 and 1977. To counteract this alarming rise in foster care rates, Congress passed the Adoption Assistance and Child Welfare Act of 1980 (PL 96-272). This act, which emphasized "permanency planning" for all children, mandated public adoption agencies either to return children to their own homes as quickly as possible or to move decisively to place them with other families on a permanent basis. One result of this policy change was to dramatically alter the population of children for whom adoption agencies were required to find permanent placements. Prior to this legislation, many children in foster care were considered difficult to place (or even "unadoptable"), and so agencies spent little time or energy trying to find suitable homes for them. With the advent of permanency planning, however, agencies were required to identify potential homes for all such children. As a result, by 1986, more than one quarter of all nonrelative adoptions in the United States involved children with special needs (National Committee for Adoption, 1989). As the frequency of these adoption placements has increased, so has interest in the placement outcomes for the children and families involved. In this chapter, we present an overview of the characteristics of children who require "special needs" adoption services and describe what is currently known about the predictors of both failure and success in these challenging adoption placements.

CHARACTERISTICS
OF WAITING CHILDREN

According to Public Law 96-272, the designation "special needs" applies to children who are over age 5 years, who are members of minority groups or sibling groups, and/or who have physical, emotional, or developmental disabilities. However, most states modify these parameters to include other characteristics that qualify a particular child for the "special needs" label. Typically, modifications include reduction of the qualifying age, presence of a learning disability diagnosis, history of child maltreatment, or even residence in foster care. Often, children may exhibit more than one characteristic.

At the inception of legally mandated permanency planning, surprisingly little was known about the prevalence of various problems among children awaiting adoption. Subsequent studies, however, have documented both the demographic characteristics and preplacement histories of these children. In a national survey of waiting children, Maza (1983) found that 73% were older than 3 years, 59% were 7 years or older, and 44% were older than 10. In addition, physical and developmental disabilities were present among one third of the children. Although emotional problems were not assessed in this study, Pinderhughes (1986) noted that a significant proportion of her sample of 33 older adoptees had emotional and behavioral problems.

One characteristic of special needs children is that they often linger in foster care for long periods prior to permanent placement. Barth and Berry (1988), for example, reported that in their sample of 120 special needs families, children typically waited an average of 27 months in foster care before being relinquished for adoption, and another 2 years between being accepted as a case by an adoption agency and the actual placement. The mean number of prerelinquishment foster placements in the sample was three. In addition, adoptive parents reported a considerable amount of preplacement trauma in their children. Eighty-two percent had a history of neglect, 60% had a history of physical abuse, and 32% experienced previous sexual abuse. Emotional and behavior problems were reported in 83% of cases, with learning disabilities also quite common (59%). Fewer children were described as having developmental (40%) or physical (33%) disabilities. This sample of families, however, included a disproportionate number of disrupted placements and therefore may have included children with greater levels of problems than might otherwise characterize the general population of special needs children awaiting adoption.

Groze (1996), in contrast, in a longitudinal study of successful special needs adoptions, collected data from a sample of 71 children that was statistically very similar to the population of children awaiting placement in Iowa. Of these youngsters, 20% were mentally retarded, with physical impairments also fairly common, including medical disabilities (21%), orthopedic disabilities (13%), and sensory impairments such as blindness and deafness (5%). Emotional and behavioral problems were the most common special needs characteristic found in the children (51%), with academic and learning disabilities also present in more than one third of the sample (35%). Children ranged from having no additional special needs (beyond older age) to having six, with a mean of approximately two. The majority of children had resided in foster placements prior to adoption (75%) or had temporary placements with relatives (18%). Just over 10% were placed from group homes or psychiatric facilities. Furthermore, although 83% of children had siblings who also required adoptive placements, only 46% of the total sample were placed in sibling pairs or groups.

With respect to children's preadoptive history of maltreatment, two thirds were victims of either confirmed or suspected physical abuse or neglect, while just over one half were identified as actual or suspected victims of sexual abuse. Interestingly, these rates of preadoptive maltreatment are lower for physical abuse and neglect, but higher for sexual abuse, than those in the Barth and Berry (1988) study, which contained large numbers of disrupted placements. In both studies, however, most children exhibited significant behavioral disturbances, underscoring the multiple problems that appear to be typical of older children requiring adoptive placement.

In summary, the evidence suggests that many children awaiting adoptive placement can be classified as "special needs" according to a variety of criteria and, in fact, often exhibit multiple problems, including stressful preadoptive histories and concurrent physical and emotional problems. Such characteristics strongly suggest that families who adopt these children have to overcome many obstacles and deal with extraordinary stressors in their efforts to establish mutually rewarding relationships with their special needs children. Not all families are able to manage this difficult transition.

DISRUPTION IN
SPECIAL NEEDS ADOPTIONS

Once adoption agencies began to place such multiproblem children in adoptive homes, not surprisingly, rates of adoption disruption and dissolution increased. As noted previously, disruption refers to a situation in which either the child is returned voluntarily by the family to the agency prior to legal finalization, or the agency removes the child from the home before legal finalization because of concerns about the type of care being received. In contrast, adoption dissolution refers to the severing of all legal ties between the parents and child after the adoption has been legally finalized. Although a considerable amount of research has been conducted on rates and correlates of adoption disruption, relatively little is known about adoptions that dissolve.

Reported disruption rates have varied considerably across studies. In the early 1970s, for example, Festinger (1986) reported that the disruption rate of adoptions in California nearly tripled from 3% to 8%. Similar phenomena were observed in other localities. In the 1980s, however, disruption rates were generally found to be higher, with rates ranging from approximately 8% in a New York City study (Festinger, 1986), to 15% in a California study (Barth & Berry, 1988), to 27% in a New England study (Partridge, Hornby, & McDonald, 1986). In summarizing this literature, Rosenthal (1993) suggests that, on average, approximately 10% to 15% of older child placements disrupt, although considerable variability has been found in the disruption rate in relation to characteristics of adopted children, adoptive families, and various social work practices.

Child Characteristics. By far the most consistent variable predicting adoption disruption is the age of the child at the time of placement, with older age associated with greater disruption risk (e.g., Barth & Berry, 1988; Festinger, 1986, 1990; Partridge et al., 1986; Rosenthal, 1993). Reviewing a number of disruption studies, Kadushin and Martin (1988) reported that the average disruption rate for families who adopted infants was only 1.9%, whereas the rate for older child placements was 11%. Across studies, it is very likely that this one variable accounts for the greatest amount of variance in adoption outcome. This finding should not be surprising, as older children are more likely to have experienced multiple residential moves and other life trauma than have younger children and to have developed emotional and behavioral problems that challenge the ability of families to successfully integrate these youngsters into their midst.

In contrast to children's age, gender is not a consistent predictor of disruption (Rosenthal & Groze, 1992), although when gender is associated with disruption, boys usually have higher percentages of troubled placements (e.g., Barth & Berry, 1988; Boneh, 1979; Nelson, 1985).

The type and degree of child problems have shown mixed effects on the likelihood of disruption. For example, cognitive and orthopedic impairments as well as developmental disabilities are only weakly associated with disruption (e.g., Boneh, 1979; Partridge et al., 1986). Conversely, emotional and behavioral problems are strongly connected to increased rates of disruption (Barth & Berry, 1988; Partridge et al., 1986; Rosenthal, Schmidt, & Conner, 1988; Sack & Dale, 1982), with externalizing behaviors such as aggression, antisocial acts (e.g., stealing, vandalizing, injuring others), sexual acting out, suicidality, enuresis, and encopresis especially predictive of placement instability.

Finally, several aspects of the child's preadoptive history have been identified as salient predictors of disruption, including longer duration in foster care (Kagan & Reid, 1986), greater number of foster placements, (Boneh, 1979; Festinger, 1986), previous disrupted placements (Barth & Berry, 1988; Nelson, 1985; Partridge et al., 1986) and experience of maltreatment (Kagan & Reid, 1986).

Family Characteristics. Family variables that have been examined with respect to their impact on adoption disruption include sociodemographic factors, such as ethnicity, socioeconomic status, and family composition as well as indexes of functioning, such as flexibility, adaptability, and expectations. Generally speaking, the pattern of results linking family variables and disruption rates is complex, and the associations are typically weak (Rosenthal, 1993; Rosenthal & Groze, 1992). Sociodemographic factors, in particular, have been shown to have inconsistent effects. Some studies have found that adoptions by minority families are, alternatively, less likely to disrupt (Rosenthal et al., 1988), equally likely to disrupt (Barth & Berry, 1988), or more likely to disrupt than adoptions by nonminority families (Partridge et al., 1986). Such contradictory findings are hard to reconcile at the present time. In contrast, higher socioeconomic status, as measured by parental occupation and education, has generally shown to have a small but significant relationship with *poorer* adoption outcomes for special needs children. For example, several studies have found that families with more highly educated parents are at greater risk for disruption than families with less educated parents (Barth & Berry, 1988; Festinger, 1990; Rosenthal et al., 1988). Similarly, greater family income has also reliably predicted increased disruption rates (Barth & Berry, 1988; Groze, 1986; Rosenthal et al., 1988). It has been suggested that working-class adoptive families may have more realistic expectations regarding future adjustment outcomes for their special needs children—especially in relation to school success and job path—and show greater tolerance for the behavioral irregularities of their children than middle-class and upper-middle-class adoptive families (Brodzinsky et al., 1995; Schmidt, Rosenthal, & Bombeck, 1988). Festinger (1986), however, has suggested that some of the variance associated with these variables may be related to the type of adoption. Specifically, foster parent adoptions, which seldom disrupt, are associated with lower parental education and family socioeconomic status than other types of adoption. Unfortunately, most studies have not analyzed the number of foster parent adoptions in their samples, so this hypothesis awaits further evaluation.

Single parenthood has also shown an inconsistent relationship with place-ment disruption, with higher rates found in some studies (Boneh, 1979; Partridge et al., 1986), but not others (Barth & Berry, 1988). In addition, the presence of other children in the home, whether adopted or nonadopted, has not consistently been associated with patterns of disruption either (Barth & Berry, 1988; Festinger, 1986; Groze, 1986; Rosenthal et al., 1988; Rosenthal & Groze, 1992). Thus, no firm judgments about family composition and the likelihood of disruption seem warranted, apart from the obvious conclusion that family structure does not seem to exert a consistently powerful effect on disruption risk.

Regarding indexes of family functioning, research has found that greater rigidity in roles, rules, and patterns of interaction is associated with increased risk for disruption (Kagan & Reid, 1986; Rosenthal et al., 1988). So too are unrealistic parental expectations. Barth (1988), for example, reported that adoptions were more likely to disrupt if a child was considerably different from what parents had desired or expected. Conversely, if parents were able to get to know the child prior to beginning the adoption process, which presumably fostered realistic expectations, placements were likely to be more stable. Finally, active involvement of the father in raising the child and supporting the mother (Westhues & Cohen, 1990) as well as the availability of adequate social support (Barth & Berry, 1988) appears to reduce the risk of placement disruption in families that adopt special needs children.

Social Work Practices. The increase in adoption of children with special needs has heightened agency attention to the provision of both preadoption background information about the child as well as postadoption support services to the adoptive family. When insufficient information about the adopted child's background is provided to the family, disruption rates are higher (Barth & Berry, 1988; Nelson, 1985). In fact, in a study by Barth and Berry (1988), inadequate parental preparation was associated with increased disruption in placements deemed "low risk," whereas provision of more complete information about a child's history was associated with mainte- nance of placements initially deemed "high risk." In addition, research has indicated that participation by adoptive parents in either preplacement or postplacement support groups is effective in lowering the risk of disruption (Feigelman & Silverman, 1983). Such services, however, are rarely utilized, even by successful adoptive parents (Groze, 1996; Rosenthal & Groze, 1992). Financial subsidies for adoption of special needs children also appear to mitigate against disruption in placement of high-risk special needs children (Barth & Berry, 1988). Finally, the use of professional support services following placement that address specific child problems (e.g., misbehavior, academic difficulties) has also been associated with greater family stability (Barth & Berry, 1988; Partridge et al., 1986; Rosenthal & Groze, 1992).

Overall, these findings indicate that well-informed and well-prepared adoptive parents are more likely to achieve successful placements than poorly informed and poorly prepared parents; however, social service agencies, for whatever reason, have difficulty engaging prospective parents in such services.

SUCCESSFUL OUTCOMES
IN SPECIAL NEEDS ADOPTIONS

Although research on adoption disruption provides valuable information on factors related to placement instability, this literature says very little about the majority of special needs adoptive families—those who are satisfied with their decision and family life and where the placement remains intact.

Research describing the strengths and healthy adaptations of special needs adoptive families has only recently been undertaken. For example, Groze (1996) and Pinderhughes and her colleagues (Pinderhughes, 1996; Pinderhughes, Leddick, Nix, & Smith, 1995) have attempted to identify variables and processes associated with positive family adjustment following adoption of a special needs child. More impressively, both investigators are evaluating adoptive family adjustment prospectively, in the context of articulated models of family functioning. Prospective research designs are preferable to retrospective studies for a variety of reasons, the most salient of which is the greater ability to attribute causation to temporally separate variables (cf. Groze, 1996). In addition, theory-driven research makes a more practical contribution to the field, as it provides a context within which researchers and clinicians can conceptualize adoptive family functioning and provides other investigators with heuristic information on which to base future work.

Pinderhughes's (1996) model is process oriented and describes a developmental sequence of stages through which families predictably move as they adapt to the inclusion of an older child. She describes four discrete stages, beginning with *anticipation,* which is concerned with the family's and child's expectations, fantasies, and advance planning prior to the child's arrival. Anticipation is succeeded by *accommodation,* which begins as soon as the child is placed and involves testing of limits and examination of the fit between expectations and reality, both by the child and the family. *Resistance,* the next stage, is not inevitable but often occurs when adoptive family members become ambivalent about the placement and try to maintain pre-adoption attitudes and behaviors despite evidence that they are dysfunctional. Finally, *restabilization* occurs when the family achieves a new equilibrium of family interaction. One important value of this model is its identification and normalization of the discordant family relations and upheavals that are often attendant on adoption of a child with special needs.

Pinderhughes and her colleagues (Pinderhughes et al., 1995) have begun a prospective examination of family functioning in special needs adoptive families in order to determine whether or not these proposed stages correspond to families' actual experiences. Investigators conducted monthly interviews and observational assessments of 11 families with special needs children, beginning one month prior to the actual placement and continuing through (at last report) 8 months postplacement. Several trends consistent with the proposed stage model have been identified. For example, family expectations during the preplacement period tended to be overly optimistic, in terms of the level of child behavior problems, and focused more on how to build a relationship with the adopted child. After the placement had occurred, families reported considerably more concerns about behavior problems and fewer concerns with relationship building. This is consistent with the model's predictions, in which families, soon after placement, begin to compare preplacement expectations with postplacement reality. Furthermore, most families demonstrated an initial decrease in functioning following placement, followed by a gradual increase over time. This pattern corresponds to predictions of the shift from the resistance to the restabilization phase. It will be interesting to note how well the families' patterns of adaptation correspond to the model's stages over longer periods. Although in its early stages, this study and others like it are certain to provide invaluable data about the adaptations that families make over time in integrating their special needs child into their lives.

Groze's (1996) model, in contrast, relies not on stages but on recognizing the complex interplay of various family subsystems within the larger context of the community. Following other theoreticians (e.g., Brodzinsky, 1987; Talen & Lehr, 1984), he asserts that adoptive families, particularly those that adopt special needs children, face unique stressors and life cycle issues that distinguish them from nonadoptive families. Consistent with family systems theory, Groze (1996) reasons that stressors may be present at the level of the larger community (e.g., adoption is not recognized to be as legitimate a means of family building as birth), the social service system (e.g., the homestudy), the family system (e.g., rigidity of functioning), and the child subsystem of the family (e.g., behavior problems). Similarly, resources may be present at all levels: positive media stories about adoption, sensitive agency personnel, skill training to enhance family adaptability, and individual or family therapy aimed at child management. In terms of understanding positive family adaptations, the degree to which available family resources balance the stressors that a given family experiences is of particular interest.

In order to assess the applicability of these concepts to special needs adoptive families, Groze conducted a four-year longitudinal study of Iowa families who had legally adopted (i.e., placements had not disrupted prior to legalization) special needs children. Throughout the study, assessment strategies designed to identify resources and stressors at each system level were incorporated. A complete summary of the study's findings is not practical here, so only relevant major points related to adoption outcomes will be highlighted. Over the course of the study, no adoptions were dissolved, and only 8% of children experienced extended out-of-home placement (such as foster care or psychiatric hospitalization). Given this pattern, it is not too surprising that these families generally reported considerable satisfaction with their decisions to adopt. Interestingly, these ratings decreased over the 4 years of the study, but still remained very positive at the study's end, with only 14% saying that the impact of the adoption on their family had been mostly or very negative. At the conclusion of the study, 84% of parents strongly agreed that they would adopt again, whereas only 20% strongly agreed that they would advise others not to adopt.

Families also reported considerable utilization of professional services (such as family therapy) over the course of the study, and utilization levels increased as the study progressed. Informal sources of support (parent support groups), however, were rarely used, but were rated positively by those who did participate in them. Families reported using professionals, not only as resources for valuable information about adoption issues, but also for emotional support during difficult times. In addition, families described high levels of support from friends and families regarding their decision to adopt a special needs child. These findings highlight the important stress-buffering role that social support, at various levels, can have for special needs families.

Groze (1996) also examined how changes over time in family and child variables were related to both parents' willingness to adopt again as well as their advising others not to adopt. Results indicated that decreases in family adaptability, improvements in parent-child communication, increases in respect from the adopted child, and increases in family income over the course of the study all were associated with parents' willingness to advise others to adopt. The child's having fewer disabilities or special needs at the study's inception was also related to positive recommendations to others regarding adoption. It is noteworthy that decreased family adaptability was apparently associated with greater willingness to recommend adoption. Groze (1996) suggests that this may reflect the construction of less chaotic, more structured boundaries in the family, reflecting the healthy incorporation of the child into the family system. In fact, families in this study scored higher than norms on measures of family adaptability at the study's outset.

In terms of predicting parental willingness to adopt again, a different set of variables seemed to be involved. Increases in family cohesion, decreases in anxious attachment behaviors on the child's part, improvements in communication, younger age at adoption placement, and absence of sexual abuse history were all significantly related to parents' judgments of their willingness to adopt another special needs child. Overall, this study provides valuable information about the aspects of family functioning that require greater attention from adoption researchers.

Finally, in reviewing research on parenting issues in special needs adoptions, Brodzinsky et al. (1995) identified five major areas associated with variability in adoption outcomes: integrating the child into the family, forming attachments and supporting the grief process, maintaining realistic expectations regarding child behavior and family functioning, managing troublesome child behavior, and utilizing supports and social services.

Integrating an older, special needs child into a family usually is less predictable and more difficult than integrating a newborn baby in a family, whether adopted or not. New roles and routines must be established, and when other children are already present, adjustments associated with trans-formation of their ordinal position in the family must be made. It is also important to recognize that special needs adopted children typically come from dysfunctional family systems and therefore may be skeptical of attempts to build family cohesion and bonding. Parents can help children through the integration process by recognizing and adapting appropriate routines from their previous placements and incorporating them into the family, by focusing on similarities between the child and new family members, and by modifying nuclear and extended family rituals to include the child.

In terms of attachment formation, it is important to recognize that children with special needs have often experienced several disrupted relationships (with biological and foster families). In turn, these experiences may interfere with the formation of healthy, secure parent-child bonds in the adoptive family. The importance of such bonds is highlighted in research suggesting that security in attachment between special needs adopted children and their adoptive parents is associated with positive adoption outcomes (Barth & Berry, 1988; Groze, 1996). Unfortunately, the process of attachment forma-tion in special needs families is still poorly understood. The application of cognitively mediated models of attachment (Main et al., 1985) to relationship development in special needs adoptive families, although promising (cf. Chisholm, Carter, Ames, & Morison, 1995), has received little attention to date. It is also especially important for adoptive parents of special needs children to maintain openness regarding the child's feelings of grief over the loss of previous attachment figures. Although many parents find such feelings threatening, reluctance to allow children to discuss these relationships may interfere with their ability to cope with such losses, which, in turn, may increase the risk for adjustment problems (Brodzinsky et al., 1995; Reitz & Watson, 1992).

The parents' ability to maintain realistic expectations regarding child behavior and family functioning is an important predictor of placement stability (Barth & Berry, 1988), especially when child characteristics do not match the family's initial desires or hopes for the child (Partridge et al., 1986). In fact, in a study comparing the parenting experiences of families who had adopted developmentally disabled children with families who had given birth to such children, Glidden (1991) found that adoptive parents reported better outcomes in terms of child, parent, and family functioning compared with birth families. These findings were attributed, in part, to the greater preparedness, and hence more realistic expectations, for child problems that had accompanied the *choice* of adopting a developmentally disabled child, as compared with the surprise, shock, and violated expectations that occurred when parents gave birth to such a child.

With respect to the management of child behavior problems, studies generally point to the positive effects of flexible styles of decision making (Kagan & Reid, 1986; Rosenthal et al., 1988) and greater level of paternal involvement in child care (Westhues & Cohen, 1990) on placement stability. In particular, parents must be prepared to deal with acting-out behaviors, emotional withdrawal, and lack of responsivity from their special needs adopted children (Rosenthal, 1993). Unfortunately, many adoptive parents find that techniques that work with other children do not seem to be effective with special needs children. These frustrationss must be offset with qualities that several authors deem essential to effective parenting of these children: tolerance for ambivalent feelings and rejection, ability to find happiness in small improvements, a sense of humor, and ability to delay parental gratification (Elbow, 1986; Katz, 1986; Rosenthal, 1993).

Finally, ongoing social services and support are essential factors in helping parents manage the challenges of special needs adoptive parenting. Some of these factors involve social work practices described previously in this chapter. Others, however, such as informal contact with other adoptive parents, involvement in adoptive parent support groups, support from extended family and friends, and proximity of relatives have been demonstrated to predict positive adoption outcomes (Barth & Berry, 1988; Rosenthal, 1993).

Successful Outcomes Among Drug Exposed Children. One aspect of special needs adoption that is gaining increased attention is the outcome of placements of children exposed prenatally to drugs and alcohol. Some authors attribute the dramatic increases in infant foster care placements primarily to this phenomenon (Wulczyn, 1994). Often, these very young children stay in foster care for prolonged periods (Barth, Courtney, Berrick, & Albert, 1994; Wulczyn, 1994). Barth and Needell (1996) speculate that one reason these children remain in care for so long is the general reluctance of adults to consider adopting children who have been prenatally exposed to drugs. This reluctance may be attributable to negative media (Blakeslee, 1990) and caseworker attitudes about the prospects of such placements. Indeed, only a few years ago, one of us was told by an adoption casework supervisor that so-called "crack babies" were essentially "nonhuman" and "another species altogether." Such accounts, however, have been based on very few empirical data (Barth & Needell, 1996).

So what do the outcome studies of drug-exposed children tell us? Initially, several studies depicted very negative outcomes, including poorly function-ing attachment behavior systems (Moore & Camarda, 1993) and "uncon-trollable" anger outbursts and defiance (Griffith, Azuma, & Chasnoff, 1994). However, these studies as well as others did not differentiate between the child's prenatal and postnatal experiences. In many cases, children prenatally exposed to drugs continued to live with their drug-involved parents after being born. Thus, the important effects of ongoing negative parental care were not adequately controlled in this research (cf. Barth & Needell, 1996). Studying children adopted into nondrug environments presents an excellent paradigm in which to examine such effects.

Barth & Needell (1996) compared child health, child behavior problems, school performance, parent satisfaction with adoption, disruption rates, and perceived emotional closeness between parents and children in families of 220 drug-exposed, 201 non-drug-exposed, and 587 unknown-drug-status adopted children participating in the California Long Range Adoption Study. Sixty-two percent of the drug-exposed children were exposed prenatally to crack cocaine, 63% to other forms of cocaine, and 59% to heroin, according to adoptive parents. Prenatal marijuana exposure was reported by 75% of adoptive parents. Assessments were made 2 and 4 years following adoptive placements. Results indicated that drug-exposed children were no more likely to be rated as having health problems than were non-drug-exposed children. Behavior problems did not significantly differ across groups overall, but the hyperactivity subscale score was higher among drug-exposed children. In addition, no differences in school grades, disobedience, or other school problems were detected. Parents in all groups reported high satisfaction with their adopted children, and no between-group differences emerged. Disrup-tion was very rare in the sample (less than 1%) and did not vary as a function of drug exposure. Finally, on ratings of emotional closeness, parents of drug-exposed children actually reported higher levels of closeness than parents of non-drug-exposed children. These results prompted the authors to conclude that drug-exposed children can overcome their early adversity and function very much like other children when they are raised in nurturing, drug-free adoptive homes. Overall, these findings stand in sharp contrast to early, poorly controlled reports and anecdotal accounts of "crack babies." Barth and Needell argue that should other investigators come to similar conclusions regarding the resilience of drug-exposed children, then adoption agencies and professionals need to help revise policies to speed up the permanent placement of drug-exposed infants who enter foster care.

SUMMARY

Special needs adoptions are on the rise, and given the ongoing problems with child maltreatment, parental drug use, and the HIV epidemic, there is no evidence to suggest that they will be substantially reduced in the near future. Although this type of adoption involves children with multiple problems, surprisingly, most placements remain intact and parents report being quite satisfied with their adoption decision. Furthermore, these children fare significantly better long-term than youngsters who continue to live in neglecting and/or abusive biological families or who linger for long periods in foster care. Although early research in this area focused primarily on actuarial concerns such as rates and correlates of adoption disruption, more recent work has begun examining family processes and models of functioning related to successful special needs placements. This shift in research focus not only is more theory driven, but is likely to have considerable practical significance for social service professionals and mental health clinicians who are seeking to help families successfully integrate special needs children into their families.

6

TRANSRACIAL AND INTERCOUNTRY ADOPTION

One of the more controversial aspects of current child welfare policy and practice concerns the appropriateness of placing children in families that differ in racial or ethnic background from the child's birth parents. Transracial adoption in the United States typically has involved placing minority children in white families. Proponents of these type of placements argue that the disproportionately large numbers of minority children who are in foster care (McRoy, Oglesby, & Grape, 1997), combined with the relative dearth of available racially matched families willing to adopt, demand that children be placed in nurturing, stable homes without respect to race. Opponents of transracial adoption, on the other hand, suggest that placement of children outside their own racial group will undermine the development of positive racial identity, ultimately leading to "cultural genocide" (Chestang, 1972; Chimezie, 1975). Critics also argue that transracial placement increases children's risk for long-term psychological problems. A second type of adoption that often, but not always, involves transracial placement is inter-country adoption, in which a child born in one country is adopted by a family in another country. This type of adoption is on the rise in the United States. Although many of the same issues about racial identity and psychological development have been raised about foreign-born children adopted by American families, there has been much less controversy in this country about this type of adoptive placement. In this chapter, we briefly summarize the history of transracial and intercountry adoption, review the arguments pro and con for such placements, especially those involving the adoption of minority children by white families, and examine research evaluating the outcome of these placements.

HISTORY OF TRANSRACIAL
AND INTERCOUNTRY ADOPTION

Transracial adoption in the United States began in the late 1940s and early 1950s, when veterans of World War II began adopting Japanese and Chinese children who had been orphaned in the war. Nearly 3,000 Japanese children and 840 Chinese children were adopted during this period, mostly by white families (Weil, 1984). As the involvement of the United States shifted from Japan and China to Korea and then Vietnam, new sources of international adoption opened up. Records indicate that between 1953 and 1981, more than 38,000 Korean children were adopted by American families (Weil, 1984). Although the Korean government took steps in 1974 to reduce the numbers of children being placed outside of their country, Silverman (1993) reported that 1,000 to 2,000 Korean children continue to be adopted by American families each year. In addition, during the United States involvement in the Vietnam War, adoption of Vietnamese children became relatively common, although such placements all but ceased with the war's end and only recently have begun again.

Not all transracial adoption in the United States has involved the placement of Asian children with American families. Since the 1960s, adoptions of children from South and Central America have been steadily increasing. Estimates from the 1980s indicate that more than 1,000 such Latino children were being adopted by American families annually, coming primarily from Colombia, El Salvador, and Mexico (Feigelman & Silverman, 1983; Weil, 1984). However, these adoptions have become increasingly difficult to arrange due to resistance of some countries to the removal of children from their culture. With the breakup of the Soviet Union and the end of the Cold War, a great deal of attention has shifted to Eastern Europe as a source of intercountry adoption. Yet even in these countries, there is evidence indicating increasing resistance to out-of-country placement. In July 1991, for example, Romania essentially shut down its international adoption program for approximately 4 months, while it developed an internal bureaucracy to handle such operations (Groze & Ileana, 1996). Most recently, attention has shifted back to China as a source of adoptable children. For the past few years, more children have been placed from China than from any other country. The availability of Chinese children for adoption is the result of their governmental policy restricting each family to one biological child. Interestingly, almost all of the Chinese children being adopted are girls, reflecting, in part, the lower status of females in that culture.

Transracial placement of minority children from within the United States first began in a systematic way with the Indian Adoption Project of the late 1950s (Fanshel, 1972). Designed to locate both intraracial and transracial homes for displaced Native American children, the project placed more than 600 children, the majority with white families. However, Native American opposition to the removal of children from their tribal communities eventually led to a dramatic reduction in these placements.

Another example of resistance to domestic transracial adoption involved the placement of African American children with white families. During the 1960s, the formation of parent and child advocacy groups, such as The Open Door Society in Canada and Parents to Adopt Minority Youth in Minnesota spurred considerable interest in adoption of African American infants by nonminority families. The rate of such placements increased sharply throughout the 1960s, causing a reformulation of placement policy, which until then had discouraged transracial adoption in general and black-white placements in particular. For example, the Child Welfare League of America issued a statement in 1968 stating that, in essence, the differing racial backgrounds of adoptive parents and children should not preclude a potential placement. With this official sanction, African American-white adoptions numbered more than 12,000 from 1960 to 1976 (Silverman & Weitzman, 1986). In the early 1970s, however, opposition from the National Association of Black Social Workers (NABSW) led to a reevaluation of the wisdom of transracial placement. The NABSW decried the "cultural genocide" (Chestang, 1972) that the placement of African American infants in white families represented, and essentially argued that such placements were "emblematic of wider historical and political injustices," such as slavery (Rushton & Minnis, 1997, p. 148). Of particular concern was the apparent lack of effort aimed at finding families within the African American community for African American children (Silverman & Feigelman, 1990). This critique of transracial placements led to another modification of agency policy, as reflected by the Child Welfare League's 1973 revision of its adoption standards. The new standards stated that children placed in in-racial adoptions were likely to be better adjusted and integrated into their communities, and that such placements were to be sought preferentially. After 1976, adoption of African American children by white families became increasingly rare (Silverman & Feigelman, 1990).

Today, rates of transracial adoptions are difficult to determine because statistics are not tabulated by any central or federal authority. Silverman and Feigelman (1990) estimate that approximately 1,000 to 2,000 minority children are adopted by white families each year in the United States. Most of these placements involve special needs youngsters of African American descent. Such special needs placements are somewhat less controversial because of the difficulty in identifying parents of any race who are willing to adopt these "hard-to-place" children. Statistics on intercountry adoption are more reliable because of the necessity for children to be processed by the Immigration and Naturalization Service when they first enter the country. Based on these records, Stolley (1993) notes that approximately 10,000 intercountry adoptions have been occurring annually over the past few years, many of which involve transracial placements. Although the majority of these youngsters are coming from countries in the Pacific Rim, Eastern Europe, and South and Central America, the internal politics of many foreign countries regarding adoption policy is constantly changing, resulting in an unpredictable pattern in the nature of intercountry placements over time.

Transracial adoption of minority infants remains highly controversial (Rushton & Minnis, 1997; Silverman & Feigelman, 1990). The NABSW and its British counterpart, the Association of Black Social Workers and Allied Professionals, maintain their ardent opposition to virtually all transracial placements, with little regard for extenuating circumstances. On the other hand, groups such as the North American Council on Adoptable Children strongly advocate transracial placements as a means of joining children with permanent families. Taking a middle position is the Child Welfare League of America, whose 1988 standards state that, although it is clearly preferable for adoptive parents and children to be racially matched, adoptions should not be "denied or significantly delayed" if an appropriate inracial placement is unavailable. Recent passage of Public Law 104-542, however, has rendered such guidelines moot. This legislation is specifically geared toward speeding up the process of adoption for children who continue to linger in foster care—many of whom are minority youngsters—by eliminating race as a barrier to a timely adoptive placment.

Transracial Placements:
Perspectives For and Against

As reviewers (e.g., Rushton & Minnis, 1997) have pointed out, two types of arguments are typically offered in opposition to the continuing practice of transracial placement. First, it is posited that minority children raised in nonminority families will suffer from a variety of adverse emotional, developmental, and/or sociocultural outcomes, especially inadequate racial identity and low self-esteem. Central to this perspective is the belief that positive racial identity is at the core of healthy personal development and that transracial adoptees, because of their inadequate racial identity, will demonstrate poorer psychological adjustment than their in-racial adopted peers. The opposing viewpoint states that outcomes in transracial adoption are not inherently negative, and that a child's need for a stable, permanent family outweighs the possible benefit that a racially matched family can make in the life of the child.

The second type of argument against transracial placement is in essence political in nature (Rushton & Minnis, 1997). The social and cultural systems that have permitted and encouraged transracial placements are thought to reflect deeply biased ideologies that fail to recognize the unique strengths of minority cultures. Accordingly, most of the arguments made against transracial placements from this perspective focus on the perceived failings of the social service system. For example, decisions that have resulted in a disproportionately large number of minority children being removed from their family of origin are believed to be based on racist or ethnocentric practices in human service agencies. Similarly, agency attempts to place such children outside the minority community are believed to reflect either lack of effort in identifying appropriate minority families or inadequately justified rejection of minority families as potential adoptive parents. Simply put, transracial placement has been viewed as a means of oppression (Association of Black Social Workers and Allied Professions, 1983).

In contrast, others argue that transracial placement is a beneficial practice because it promotes racial integration, the ideal toward which an enlightened society should strive (Hayes, 1993). Similarly, some critics (e.g., Bartholet, 1993b) have argued that adoption policies that prohibit transracial placement are, themselves, racially discriminatory and therefore violate laws protecting civil rights. According to this perspective, social service policies that permit transracial adoption cannot be considered racist, as they do not recognize the superiority of any race in terms of the ability to provide nurturing homes for children.

The debate over transracial adoption is complex, emotional, and value-laden. Given the strong positions taken by each side, and the significant policy implications of the arguments being made, it would seem logical to assume that such controversy would produce considerable research aimed at resolving these issues. Surprisingly, however, there is relatively little research on the specific outcomes of transracial placements. In the next section, we will examine what is known about the impact of transracial placement on adoption stability and children's adjustment.

OUTCOME IN
TRANSRACIAL ADOPTION

Research, to date, has unfortunately failed to provide definitive answers to many of the central questions about the practice of transracial adoption. This is due, in part, to a simple dearth of studies as well as to methodological problems characterizing the bulk of research in this area. In addition, most research has focused on the adoption of African American infants by white families, to the exclusion of other types of transracial placements, which have become increasingly common in recent years. Although some research has addressed other forms of transracial placement (e.g., Andujo, 1988; Bausch & Serpe, 1997; Feigelman & Silverman, 1983), our knowledge about these types of families is quite limited. Thus, policymakers looking to make empirically based decisions regarding transracial placement must rely on meager and sometimes contradictory data.

Stability of Transracial Placements

Research has been nearly unanimous in failing to find disproportionately large disruption or dissolution rates among transracial placements (Barth & Berry, 1988; Boneh, 1979; Festinger, 1986; Partridge et al., 1986). Barth and Berry, for example, examined adoption disruption among families of 927 California children who were placed after their third birthday. The authors reported an overall disruption rate of 10.2%. Although the percentage of transracial placements in this sample was not large (only 19%), no differences in disruption rate were found between transracial and in-racial placements. Furthermore, although Charles, Rashid, and Thoburn (1992) did find greater rates of disruption among transracial adoptions in Great Britain, this finding was accounted for by the older age at placement of the transracial sample. Thus, the argument that the stress of adopting across racial lines will inevitably cause families to terminate placements is not supported by available data.

Psychological Adjustment in
Transracial Adopted Children

Critics of transracial adoption have also expressed concern that these children will be at greater risk for a variety of psychological problems than children placed within their own race. This issue has been addressed empirically in several ways. At the most general level, a number of studies have examined "overall adjustment" in transracial adoption, at times combining data derived from parents, teachers, and children themselves, and found that, by and large, the vast majority of these youngsters demonstrate satisfactory adjustment (e.g., Andujo, 1988; Fanshel, 1972; Grow & Shapiro, 1974; McRoy & Zurcher, 1983; Shireman & Johnson, 1986; Simon & Altstein, 1977, 1987). For example, two early studies using similar methods (parent interviews) and dependent measures (composite ratings) found that 75% of Native American children (Fanshel, 1972) and 77% of African American children (Grow & Shapiro, 1974) raised in white families exhibited normal to excellent developmental outcomes.

Subsequent studies have improved somewhat on the experimental rigor of these early descriptive investigations and have yielded similar results. Simon and Altstein (1977, 1987), for example, conducted a longitudinal investigation of more than 200 transracial adoptees placed by private agencies. Both adoptive parents and children were interviewed three times over 11 years, and psychological test data were collected from the adoptees and their nonadopted siblings. Most adoptions involved the placement of African American children with white families, but children from other minority groups were also included. Interview data indicated that parents expressed considerable satisfaction in their roles as adoptive parents across the span of the study, and that adoptees felt strongly attached to their adoptive families (Simon & Altstein, 1987). Among the follow-up data was a measure of self-esteem completed by the adoptees and their siblings. No differences were evident across groups of African American adoptees, transracial adoptees from other minority groups, and nonadopted siblings.

Comparable results were found by McRoy and Zurcher (1983). However, the researchers designed this study so that a comparison of transracial and in-racial adoptive status was possible. They interviewed 30 white and 30 African American families who had all adopted African American children. Included among the measures was the Tennessee Self-Concept Scale, on which both in-racial and transracial adoptees produced similar scores. In addition, scores from both groups were quite similar to normative scores of nonadopted white children. McRoy and Zurcher (1983) interpreted their results to suggest that in-racial adoption was not necessary for the development of healthy self-esteem.

Thus, at the level of general adjustment, the bulk of the data indicate that transracially adopted children do not suffer negative developmental outcomes, nor do they have negative self-images. These results, however, do not address the greatest concern raised with regard to transracial adoption—

namely, whether this type of placement is likely to interfere with the development of healthy racial attitudes and racial identity.

Racial Identity in Transracial Adopted Children

Studies that have attempted to investigate racial identity among transracially adopted children have been plagued by a number of conceptual and methodological problems, with the resulting empirical picture being far from clear.

At the conceptual level, there has been little agreement among investigators on the definition of "racial identity" (DeBerry, Scarr, & Weinberg, 1996; Rushton & Minnis, 1997). Some authors consider racial identity to be a stable personal characteristic, such as personality type, while others have argued that an individual's racial attitudes are changeable and even situation-specific (DeBerry et al., 1996; Rushton & Minnis, 1997). Different conceptualizations have profound implications for how this construct is operationalized in research. To date, racial identity has been assessed by a variety of methods, including parental reports, projective tests, and even expressed preferences for living in certain types of neighborhoods. The lack of a consistent operational definition of racial identity likely explains the diversity in research strategies as well as the observed discrepancies in results across studies.

Grow and Shapiro (1974) assessed the degree to which adoptive parents thought it was important for their children to identify with, and participate in, "black culture." The great majority of parents deemed it to be very important, and higher levels of parental support for a child's identification with the black community were associated with more positive composite child adjustment ratings made by interviewers. However, even among those parents with the most supportive attitudes toward children's identification with their racial heritage, only 49% reported that their own children had positive attitudes about their black heritage. Of those parents with the least supportive cultural attitudes, only 26% reported that their children had positive racial attitudes about being black. Although these percentages seem distressingly low, it is difficult to interpret these findings because the researchers did not include comparison groups of in-racially adopted and nonadopted African American children. Furthermore, even if the findings are valid, they may only reflect prevailing social attitudes toward minority groups in the early 1970s, when the study was conducted, and not be generalizable to the present. Finally, there is also reason to question the validity of the parental reports of racial identity, as children may be reluctant to discuss such issues with their white parents (Rushton & Minnis, 1997).

Other investigators have worked directly with children, evaluating racial identity through projective assessment measures such as the Doll Preference Test (Shireman & Johnson, 1986; Simon & Altstein, 1977). In this procedure, children are shown dolls of their own and different racial groups and asked to identify the doll they think is most attractive, least attractive, etc. The preferences are presumed to reflect the degree to which children have positive attitudes and feelings about their own versus other racial groups. In nonadopted samples, young, minority children often display preferences for white dolls over those of their own race, which has been interpreted as an internalization of societal prejudice against minorities. Shireman and Johnson (1986) compared African American children placed in-racially with those placed transracially and found that the majority of the in-racial group shifted their early preference for white dolls to black dolls by the time they were 8 years old. The transracially adopted sample, however, did not show the same change over time, and roughly 30% continued to prefer white dolls at age 8 years. This finding suggests that transracially adopted children exhibit a more negative view of their racial status, presumably as the result of being raised in white families.

Simon and Altstein (1977), however, used a similar procedure with a larger sample and found that, not only did the transracially adopted 3- to 8-year-old participants not demonstrate a preference for white over black dolls, but neither did their nonadopted white siblings. This result suggests that the presence of an African American child in the home may increase the acceptance of minority group members to majority group children. Although these findings stand in contrast to those of Shireman and Johnson (1986), there is a question of what the doll preference test actually measures and whether it is a valid indicator of racial attitudes and/or identity (cf. Rushton & Minnis, 1997)

Finally, McRoy and her colleagues (McRoy, Zurcher, Lauderdale, & Anderson, 1982), using the same sample described in the McRoy and Zurcher (1983) study, interviewed both parents and children about racial identity issues. White parents of transracially adopted children tended to avoid identifying their children as "black," whereas the African American parents of in-racially adopted children did not. This pattern was also evident in the children themselves, as a greater number of transracially placed children identified themselves as "biracial" compared with the in-racial sample. These results could be interpreted as a rejection of the African American racial identity by those children raised in white families. However, the overall pattern of results also is consistent with the conclusion that parents of transracial adoptees who accept their child's racial identification, and who do not isolate their children from the black community (i.e., live in integrated neighborhoods, send their children to integrated schools), raise children who a have positive view of themselves as African American.

One question that the above studies failed to address is whether racial identity has any bearing on the adjustment of children adopted transracially. Recently, DeBerry et al. (1996) reanalyzed data from 88 participants in the longitudinal Minnesota Transracial Adoption Project (Scarr & Weinberg, 1976) to examine the impact of various types of racial identification on interviewer ratings of psychological adjustment. Using a variety of sophisticated data analysis procedures, the researchers concluded that transracial adoptees' psychological difficulties increased over the duration of the study. Concomitantly, adoptee identification with Eurocentric values increased, whereas identification with Africentric values decreased. Decreased adjustment appeared to be related to the decrease in Africentric cultural beliefs, which were in turn related to the ways in which adoptive families handled issues of racial identification over the course of development. Data also indicated that identification with different cultural beliefs became more dichotomous over time, suggesting that families and adoptees had difficulty integrating different racial value systems as the children got older. Although the data analysis strategy used in this study may have been less than ideal for the small sample size, and the measurement of several important constructs was limited by the secondary analysis of an extant data set, this study makes an important contribution to the conceptualization of racial variables in adoption research. It is difficult to find fault with the authors' conclusion that it is less useful to discuss whether transracial adoption (especially adoption of African American children by white families) is positive or negative than whether it is possible to predict under what conditions, and at what developmental stages, problems might arise.

In conclusion, effects of transracial adoption on racial identity remain elusive. As Rushton & Minnis (1997) have pointed out, longitudinal data on the long-term functioning of transracially adopted children would be tremendously beneficial in assessing the predictive validity of the various measures of racial identity that have been assessed in childhood. The absence of clearly demonstrated negative outcomes following transracial placement, at least in the childhood and adolescent years, has led some social scientists to call for an end to agency policies discouraging such placements (Silverman & Feigelman, 1990). However, other reviewers, who have come to similar conclusions regarding the research data, continue to be very hesitant about transracial placements, based on philosophical and social value grounds (Rushton & Minnis, 1997). Clearly, improved research data are not the only missing pieces in helping child welfare agencies to formulate sound policy. Decisions based on shared values and desired cultural outcomes must also be taken into account.

OUTCOME IN
INTERCOUNTRY ADOPTION

As noted previously, significant numbers of children born in other countries have been adopted by North American families. In many cases, but not all, these adoptions involve transracial placements. A sizable percentage of these children also have special needs. Language differences between children and adoptive parents pose an additional barrier, at least initially, to successful family integration in these placements.

Although there has been concern about the outcome of intercountry adoptions, relatively little research has been conducted in this area. The work that has been done has focused on two principal issues: children's medical status and psychosocial adjustment. Generally, both indexes have revealed positive outcomes for internationally adopted children, although some problems have been noted associated primarily with preadoption experiences of children in their countries of origin.

In terms of medical outcomes, there has been much attention devoted to the presence of various infectious diseases (e.g., hepatitis B, tuberculosis, sexually transmitted disease) in children adopted from other countries (DeVoid, Pineiro-Carrerro, Goodman, & Latimer, 1992; Gyorkos & MacLean, 1992; Hostetter et al., 1991). Such conditions are often identified prior to adoption, providing parents with advance knowledge of what types of treatment to seek and precautions to take to prevent the spread of disease. In other cases, however, parents are unprepared for health complications, which can greatly increase the stress associated with adoption (Miller, Kiernan, Mathers, & Klein-Gitelman, 1995; Smith-Garcia & Brown, 1989). In the majority of cases, the diseases found in intercountry adoptees are treatable or manageable and do not cause prolonged hardship for the child or family (Smith-Garcia & Brown, 1989).

Apart from infectious disease, malnutrition and digestive problems have often been noted. Intestinal parasites are especially common (Miller et al., 1995; Smith-Garcia & Brown, 1989), although treatments for this condition are well known and generally effective. Most effects of malnutrition can be overcome with improvements in diet; however, there are long-term consequences associated with nutritional problems during infancy and early childhood. Development of the hippocampus, cerebellum, and stress response centers of the brain may be impaired by early malnutrition (Levitsky & Strupp, 1995). Furthermore, there is some indication that a commonly observed phenomenon in intercountry adoptees—early onset of puberty—may be related to nutritional changes (Bourguignon et al., 1992). These observations have led several authors to urge parents of international adoptees to obtain thorough medical examinations as soon as possible, even if previous medical examinations were conducted, because such preadoption examinations often overlook important problems (Johnson et al., 1992).

With respect to psychosocial adjustment of intercountry adoptees, results are also quite positive. This is particularly true of children adopted from Asian countries such as China, Korea, and Vietnam (Bagley, 1993; Dalen & Saetersdal, 1987; Kim, 1995). Generally, research has found intercountry adoptees to be functioning at average to above-average levels in academic, psychological, and vocational domains, across all ages studied. These outcomes are particularly evident when intercountry adoptees are compared with the general population. Other comparison groups have shown similar but slightly different results. In one study, for example, adolescent and adult international (mostly Asian) adoptees were performing well compared with general population controls, but lower than their nonadopted siblings on some indexes of psychological adjustment (Cohen & Westhues, 1995). Furthermore, in research that has found greater problems among international adoptees compared with their nonadopted peers, the results are largely accounted for by variables such as older age at placement and preplacement social adversity (e.g., neglect, abuse, institutional rearing) rather than adoption status per se (Verhulst et al., 1990, 1992).

Problems in preplacement child rearing have been the focus of much attention for one group of international adoptees—Romanian children—who have shown signficant postadoption adjustment problems. At the beginning of this decade, news coverage of the post-revolution social conditions in Romania spurred considerable interest in the welfare of children living in state-sponsored orphanages and other institutions. Soon after, many North American parents sought and successfully adopted Romanian children, as the process was not well controlled and could be accomplished relatively quickly and easily (Groze & Ileana, 1996). The lure of money apparently was quite tempting for "baby brokers," and it was not long before the situation became exploitative and dehumanizing (Johnson & Groze, 1993), leading to a temporary cessation of Romanian adoptions in 1991. As the number of adoptions began to decrease following the 1991 moratorium, greater attention was paid to the adjustment of children who had already been adopted. Initial reports were alarming, with very serious medical, developmental, and attachment problems described (Chisolm et al., 1995; Marcovitch, Cesaroni, Roberts, & Swanson, 1995; Morison, Ames, & Chisolm, 1995). For example, adoptive parents of Romanian children described their youngsters, in the first few months following placement, as demonstrating a variety of problems with feeding and sleeping, significant medical difficulties, serious developmental delays in social behavior, resistance to attachment, and frequent high-level tantrum behavior (Marcovitch et al., 1995). Three years post-adoption, many problems had diminished, but medical problems, social-developmental problems, and temper tantrums remained serious. This study also compared children adopted from orphanages with those adopted from birth parents; findings indicated that those adopted from orphanages showed the greatest disturbances across domains.

Similarly, in a series of studies, Ames, Chisolm, and their colleagues (Chisolm et al., 1995; Fisher, Ames, Chisolm, & Savoie, 1997; Morison et al., 1995) compared adopted children who had spent at least 8 months in Romanian orphanages with both never-adopted, never-institutionalized Canadian-born children, and age- and sex-matched Romanian children who were adopted prior to 4 months of age (and who would have been institutionalized in Romania had they not been adopted). These studies consistently found that the institutionalized adopted children showed greater gross motor, adaptive, social, and language delays; had greater attachment problems; and displayed greater total, and internalizing, behavior problems than either the Canadian or never-institutionalized Romanian children. These authors suggested that neglect and possible abuse associated with orphanage life probably was the cause for the variety of problems these children exhibited. Fisher et al. (1997) suggests, however, that with ongoing stimulation and nurturance by adoptive parents, these children are likely to continue to improve over time.

Groze and Ileana (1996) also provide an optimistic picture for the outcome of previously institutionalized Romanian children. Using a mailed questionnaire, these authors surveyed 475 parents of adopted Romanian children, which accounted for approximately 16% of all Romanian adoptions that occurred between 1990 and 1993. Although the researchers did not find a relationship between length of time in institutional care and adjustment among Romanian adoptees, there was a clear, positive relationship between any institutional placement and almost all developmental and behavior problems that were assessed. Despite experiencing numerous problems with their children, more than 75% of the parents reported that the adoption had a "very positive" impact on the family. Furthermore, 93% of parents reported that they "never" consider ending the adoptive placement. Thus, adoption outcome, from the parents' perspective, was not associated with their children's preplacement institutional experiences. On the other hand, expressed parental dissatisfaction with adoption was associated with lack of preparation for adoptive parenthood. Specifically, those parents who had not been primed to anticipate problems were also the ones who found the adoptions to be least satisfactory. Overall, however, the authors conclude that, in contrast to some early reports, "cautious optimism" does seem warranted regarding the potential for success of children who have experienced preplacement institutional life.

SUMMARY

Transracial adoptions began as a means of providing orphans from war-ravaged countries with loving parents, but gradually expanded to include minority group children from within our borders and as a result grew increasingly controversial, spurring several changes in adoption policies. The rhetoric concerning transracial placements has been highly emotionally charged, but the research base has not developed adequately to answer many of the central questions about the potential benefits and drawbacks of such placements. The data regarding racial identity are especially equivocal. Furthermore, many of the ultimate questions about transracial placement are not questions that research can answer. Rather, they are about social values and the ethics of agency practices and consequently will require a different forum for resolution than scientific journals.

Although less rhetoric has been generated about intercountry adoption than domestic transracial adoption, some of the same questions about values and ethics can be raised about these types of placements. However, these issues, as we have noted, are beyond the scope of social science researchers, whose primary goal is to study the outcome of these adoptions. To date, the bulk of the data suggest that children placed outside their country of origin into adoptive families generally do quite well, despite the fact that they are at risk for a variety of medical conditions and often experience institutional rearing. These results point, once again, to the protective function of adoption in the lives of children who have suffered early biological and social adversity.

7

OPEN ADOPTION

In the first half of this century, adoption practice in this country was based, to a large extent, on three primary principles: secrecy, anonymity, and sealing of records. Adoption agencies went to great lengths to prevent birth parents and adoptive parents from meeting one another and sharing identifying information. At the time of adoption, all records of the proceeding, including the original birth certificate, were sealed by court order, and an amended birth certificate for the child was issued to the adoptive parents. These confidential adoption practices, which were supported by statutory law, were instituted by social workers in the belief that they would protect the child from the stigma of illegitimacy, preserve the birth mother's anonymity, protect her from the stigma of out-of-wedlock pregnancy, and maintain the privacy and integrity of the adoptive family.

In the 1960s and 1970s, however, a growing discontent could be heard among members of the adoption triad as well as among some adoption professionals. Questions concerning the impact of secrecy and the sealing of adoption records on the adjustment of adoptees and birth parents were being raised (Sorosky et al., 1978). In addition, an increasing number of adult adoptees and birth parents were returning to agencies and requesting additional background information and, in some cases, seeking to reunite with one another. Fueled by numerous societal changes, especially the civil rights movement and the passage of the Freedom of Information Act, a small, but vocal, group of individuals in the adoption field began to challenge the fundamental principles underlying confidential adoption (Baran, Sorosky, & Pannor, 1974; Pannor, Sorosky, & Baran, 1974). Some professionals went so far as to suggest that open adoption be standard practice for adoption agencies (Pannor & Baran, 1984). Over the past three decades, these initial pioneers in open adoption have gathered substantial support within the adoption community and have had a major impact on the way adoption is practiced in the United States today.

There is little doubt that adoption, as a social service field, is moving decidedly toward increased openness, and that agencies are offering a wider array of placement options for birth parents and adoptive parents (Grotevant & McRoy, 1998). The move toward greater openness, however, has not been without controversy. There are strong critics of this type of adoption (Kraft, Palombo, Mitchell, Woods, & Schmidt, 1985a; Kraft, Palombo, Woods, Mitchell, & Schmidt, 1985b; Kraft, Palombo, Woods, Schmidt, & Tucker, 1985; Bevan & Pierce, 1994) who warn of unknown dangers and pitfalls and who point out that we know very little about how open adoption affects birth parents, adoptive parents, and especially adopted children. In this chapter, we examine some of the expectations and concerns about the influence of open adoption on children and the adoptive family and review the few empirical studies that have been conducted in this area. Readers interested in a more detailed account of the open adoption literature, and especially its impact on birth parents, should consult Berry (1993) and Grotevant and McRoy (in press).

What is Open Adoption?

Complicating our understanding of this area is a lack of consensus about how to define open adoption. Some professionals have suggested that open adoption involves direct contact between birth parents and adoptive parents, with full mutual sharing of identifying information, a plan for some type of ongoing contact between the parties, and, in many cases, selection of the adoptive family by the birth parents (Baran & Pannor, 1993). Others have emphasized that open adoption is best understood as a continuum of mutual knowledge, communication, and contact that is highly variable from family to family and subject to change over time (Grotevant & McRoy, 1998).

At one end of the openness continuum are adoption plans in which birth parents and the adoptive family not only know one another's name and location, but also include ongoing, direct contact between the parties, including the child. The frequency and nature of contact will vary from family to family. In some cases, the parties will visit in each other's homes; in other cases, there will be contact only in public places. For some families, the contact will be an ongoing part of everyday life; for others, it will be restricted to special occasions, a few times a year. Some open adoption arrangements will exclude the child from the contact plan, at least for a period of time agreed on by the parties. Other arrangements will involve direct contact, primarily or exclusively through letters and telephone calls. Plans that involve somewhat less openness typically include the use of an intermediary—usually the adoption agency or adoption attorney—to facilitate communication. In such cases, the parties may have a considerable amount of background information but usually will not know one another's identity. Often, letters, photographs, and gifts are exchanged through the intermediary, in some cases on an ongoing basis, in other cases for only a short period of time. Finally, at the other end of the openness continuum is the traditional, confidential adoption arrangement in which minimal information is provided to birth parents and adoptive parents about the other party, and in which there is no plan for updating of information over the years.

What is often not appreciated, however, is that adoption arrangements established at the time of placement very often change over time. This can occur for many reasons and be instituted by either the birth family or the adoptive family. Mendenhall, Grotevant, and McRoy (1996) found that the level of openness between the families tended to increase over time when there was unimpeded communication between the parties, when the parties had established a mutually satisfying relationship, and when there was a mutual belief that it would benefit the child. Decreased openness over time was associated with increased geographical distance between the parties; lack of support from families and friends regarding openness; lack of comfort between the parties based on major differences in life circumstances, interests, and/or values; difficulty in negotiating a mutually satisfying openness plan; and failure of the intermediary to carry out a contact plan to everyone's satisfaction.

In short, open adoption means different things to different people. From our perspective, however, the notion of an openness continuum seems most useful. As clinicians, we have been particularly impressed by the mutable nature of adoption triad family relationships. What Mendelhall et al. (1996) have documented in their research, we have witnessed in our clinical work with families—the dynamic and, at times, unpredictable evolution of intricate connections between biological and adoptive families members. Thus, it must be kept in mind that whatever adoption plan is agreed on at the time of placement, it is likely to be influenced by numerous factors and quite possibly will change in form over time.

Proposed Benefits and Risks of Open Adoption

Much has been written about the possible benefits and drawbacks of open adoption. Those individuals writing in this area, however, have been guided more by clinical and casework experience as well as by personal beliefs and biases than by empirical data. In fact, very little research has been conducted on correlates and outcomes of open adoption. Moreover, the few studies that have been published tend to suffer from serious methodological flaws, including small and potentially biased samples, inadequate control groups, use of questionable measurement instruments, and failure to control for a host of confounding variables, such as age at placement, preplacement experiences, and family structural variables (see Berry, 1993 and Grotevant & McRoy, 1998, for reviews of this research).

Opponents of open adoption have argued that greater contact between birth parents and adoptive family members may well increase the adoptive parents' insecurity, diminish their sense of control, undermine their sense of entitlement to the child, and weaken parent-child attachments (Kraft et al., 1985b). They also have argued that it may prolong the grief process for the birth mother, making it difficult for her to "get on with her life." In addition, some authors have suggested that the option of making an open adoption placement may lead some birth parents to relinquish their child when they otherwise would not do so. Cocozzelli (1989) suggests that in such cases unmet expectations regarding contact with their child could create considerable difficulty for the birth parent, resulting in greater postplacement adjustment problems. Finally, critics of open adoption have expressed concern that children in these arrangements will show increased confusion and fear, have greater difficulty forming secure bonds to their adoptive parents, manifest more identity problems, and exhibit more maladjusted behavior (Byrd, 1988; Kraft et al., 1985).

In contrast, those individuals favoring open adoption believe that the elimination of secrecy in the adoption system is likely to create a more realistic and empathic view of the birth parents by adoptive family members, thereby reducing the tendency to deny or pathologize the child's biological heritage. Baran and Pannor (1993) note that "knowing the birth parents of their children can prevent the fears and fantasies that might otherwise have a negative effect on their relationships with their adopted children" (pp. 122-123). Thus, contrary to the critics of open adoption, those favoring it believe that this type of arrangement is likely to increase the sense of control and security for adoptive parents (Chapman, Dorner, Silber, & Winterberg, 1987a). Proponents of open adoption also believe that it will diminish, not prolong, the grief and postplacement adjustment problems of the birth mother, especially if she is given greater control over who adopts her child (Baran & Pannor, 1993; Chapman, Dorner, Silber, & Winterberg, 1986). Having such control is believed to help some birth mothers make an adoption plan for their baby, when otherwise they might feel too ambivalent or guilty to do so (Barth, 1987). Finally, it has been suggested that in eliminating the secrecy and anonymity associated with adoption, open placement plans are likely to benefit children by fostering more realistic and empathic perceptions of their birth parents and the circumstances of the relinquishment. In such a situation, it is expected that children will experience adoption as less of a rejection, feel better about themselves and their connection to two families, develop a more stable identity, and have fewer adjustment problems (Baran & Pannor, 1993; Chapman, Dorner, Silber, & Winterberg, 1987b). Some authors have even suggested that living within an open adoption system is likely to facilitate an earlier and deeper understanding of adoption (Silber & Dorner, 1990).

As noted above, much rhetoric has been offered by each side of the open adoption controversy. In the section that follows, we examine what research has uncovered about the impact of this type of adoption arrangement on children and their adoptive families.

Impact of Open Adoption on
Adoptive Parents and Their Children

The few studies that have been conducted, to date, on outcomes of open adoption generally have not supported the concerns and dire warnings of open adoption critics. In a study of 1,396 infant and older child adoptions, Berry (1991) reported that children who had contact with birth parents were rated more favorably in terms of behavior by their adoptive parents than children who had no contact with birth parents. Adoptive parents in open arrangements also had more positive views of their child's birth parents than those in closed arrangements.

Several studies have shown that adoptive parents who choose open adoption generally are quite satisfied with the placement plan and have positive relationships with birth parents (Belbas, 1987; Etter, 1993; Gross, 1993; Meezan & Shireman, 1985). They also experience a greater sense of entitlement to their child (Belbas, 1987; McRoy & Grotevant, 1988; Siegel, 1993) and worry less about the birth parents reclaiming their youngster (Belbas, 1987). In addition, Silverstein and Demick (1994) found that adoptive parents in open adoptions had a more empathic view of the birth mother, worried less about attachment to their child, and viewed their child as less demanding and bothersome. However, these investigators found no difference between open and closed adoption groups in life satisfaction, life stress, and general adjustment.

Ongoing contact between children and their birth parents is reasonably common in older child adoptions. In a study of 120 special needs adopted children, Nelson (1985) reported that 20% of these youngsters remained in contact with their birth families following the adoption. In these type of placements, adoptive parents' comfort regarding contact between their children and the birth family, or previous foster parents, appears to be tied to their feelings of control over the contact (Barth & Berry, 1988; Berry, 1991). The more control they feel, the more comfortable they are. Berry (1993) also found that adoptive parents were more comfortable with open adoption when they had planned from the very beginning for an open arrangement and had talked to the birth mother prior to placement. In addition, Berry noted greater comfort with open adoption among adoptive parents when the adoptive mother was older, when the birth mother had a higher education level, and when there was an absence of abuse or neglect in the child's history.

Despite the generally positive findings, Siegel (1993) noted that adoptive parents in open arrangements did experience uncertainty about the impact of openness on their children. They also worried about the lack of social norms for their family structure as well as about the emotional demands of the relationship with the birth mother and possible rejection by her.

Perhaps the best designed, and most comprehensive, study of open versus closed adoption, to date, has been conducted by Grotevant and McRoy (1998; see also Christian, McRoy, Grotevant, & Bryant, in press; Grotevant, McRoy, Elde, & Fravel, 1994; Mendenhall et al., 1996; Wrobel, Ayers-Lopez, Grotevant, McRoy, & Friedrick, 1996). The subjects, recruited from 35 adoption agencies located across the United States, included 190 adoptive couples, 171 adopted children ranging from 4 to 12 years of age, and 169 birth mothers. The vast majority of participants were white, Protestant, and middle to upper-middle class. The study was restricted to in-racial, infant placed children. Four variations in openness were identified by the investigators: *confidential placements* (C), in which no information was shared between the adoptive parents and birth parents after 6 months postplacement (62 adoptive families); *time-limited mediated placements* (TLM), in which information was shared between the parties through the use of the adoption agency, but in which the information sharing had stopped by the time the participants were interviewed (17 adoptive families); *ongoing mediated placements* (OM), in which the exchange of information between the two families through the agency was continuing at the time of the interview (52 adoptive families); and *fully disclosed placements* (FD), in which there was direct sharing of information, usually involving face-to-face meetings, between adoptive parents and birth parents (57 adoptive families). Data were collected from all members of the adoption triad through in-depth interviews and questionnaires. For current purposes, only outcome data related to adoptive parents and adopted children will be reviewed.

For adoptive parents, 10 variables related to adoptive family dynamics were identified and coded from interview and questionnaire data:

1. communication with the child about adoption;
2. empathy toward the child;
3. empathy toward the birth parent;
4. acknowledgment that adoptive parenting is different from biological parenting;
5. acknowledgment of the child's interest in his or her background;
6. fear that the birth parent will reclaim the child;
7. adoptive parents' satisfaction with their control over the birth parent's involvement in their family life;
8. adoptive parents' sense of entitlement to act as the child's "full" parent;
9. adoptive parent's sense of permanence regarding the parent-child relationship; and
10. the degree to which the adoptive parent's philosophy about adoption is internally consistent and free of contradictions.

Results indicated that for many of these dimensions, adoptive parent attitudes and behavior varied by level of openness. For example, compared with parents from less open adoption arrangements, parents in fully disclosed adoptions generally communicated more with their child about adoption, displayed more empathy toward their child as well as toward the birth parent, showed greater acknowledgment of their child's interest in his or her background, were less fearful that their child would be reclaimed by the birth parents, were more confident of the permanence of the parent-child relationship, and displayed more coherence in the way they viewed adoption. These differences were particularly striking when comparing parents from fully disclosed adoptions with those parents from confidential adoptions. On the other hand, no differences were found among openness groups in terms of adoptive parents' sense of control regarding the birth parents' involvement in their lives, the extent to which they acknowledged adoptive parenting as different from biological parenting, and their sense of entitlement to their child.

In analyzing the relationship between children's attitudes and behavior and openness level, Grotevant, McRoy and their colleagues defined openness from three perspectives:

1. the four family openness categories—C, TLM, OM, and FD;
2. children's perception of openness, defined in terms of their knowledge of, and contact with, birth parents; and

3. whether children were included or excluded from information and/or contact by their adoptive parents.

Four primary outcome measures were examined: children's satisfaction with their level of openness; children's curiosity about their birth parents; children's understanding of adoption; and children's self-esteem. Results indicated that the extent of openness experienced by children generally was unrelated to their satisfaction with openness, their curiosity regarding birth parents, and their self-esteem. On average, younger children tended to be more satisfied with their level of openness, but less curious about their birth parents, than older children. Girls also were more curious than boys regarding their birth parents. Finally, although children's understanding of adoption did not differ among the four family openness categories or as a function of their perception of openness, adoption knowledge was greater for those children who were included in all forms of contact with the birth family compared with those youngsters who were excluded from one or more types of contact.

Although an important contribution to the open adoption literature, the research by Grotevant and McRoy has several limitations that must be noted. First, sample size was modest and the array of outcome measures employed, especially regarding children's adjustment, was rather limited. Second, the sample was restricted to infant placed children from primarily middle- to upper-middle-class white families. Generalization of the findings to other types of adoption remains unclear. In addition, although a second wave of data collection is under way (Grotevant, personal communication), the findings reported, so far, represent adjustment outcomes within a limited time period. It is quite possible that different levels of contact with birth family members would affect adopted children in different ways, depending on the developmental level at which it occurs. For example, ready and controllable access to the birth family may have more direct benefits for adolescents as they struggle to understand who they are in the context of their dual connection to two families (see Grotevant, 1997). Finally, the primary way in which openness was defined in this study—i.e., the four family openness categories— does not control whether children are included in the contact plan or the amount of contact they have with birth family members. To the extent that openness is defined primarily in terms of contact between adoptive parents and biological parents, whatever influence openness has on the child must be understood to be indirect—i.e., mediated by the attitudes and behaviors of adoptive parents. Perhaps that is the reason the current study found little influence of openness on children's attitudes and adjustment. More direct measures of the nature and frequency of contact between children and birth parents might find a stronger influence of openness on children's behavior and development.

SUMMARY

Although critics of open adoption have issued strong warnings and made dire predictions about the impact of this type of family arrangement on adoptive parents and their children, the data, to date, do not support their position. For adoptive parents, in fact, the findings suggest generally beneficial effects of increased openness. Adoptive parents who choose a more open adoption arrangement appear both satisfied with their choice and more accessible and empathic in their communication with their child about adoption, including issues related to the birth family. They also show a stronger sense of permanence regarding the parent-child relationship and less often fear that the birth parents will seek to reclaim their youngster. Thus, contrary to the critics of open adoption, this type of placement plan appears to increase the security of adoptive parents, not diminish it.

For children, however, the picture is not so clear. Although Berry (1991) found fewer behavior problems in children having more contact with the birth family, the work of Grotevant and McRoy (1998) generally found little difference in children's adjustment as a function of openness. As the latter researchers note, their findings support neither the grave warnings of adjustment problems in adoptees raised by open adoption critics, nor the hopeful expectations of open adoption supporters that greater openness will readily offset the adjustment difficulties often found in children in more closed placements.

Although clearly much more research is needed in the area of open adoption, we cannot help but think that too many adoption professionals and researchers have been focusing on the wrong question. Rather than seeking to determine which type of adoption plan—open or closed—is best for most people, it would appear more sensible to examine the benefits and drawbacks of various types of placement options, especially at different developmental and family life cycle phases. Grotevant and McRoy (1998) emphasize that contact plans between adoptive and birth families often change over time, reflecting evolving personal needs and life circumstances. Thus, it seems rather shortsighted to expect that any one type of placement plan is likely to meet most people's needs all of the time. From our perspective, adoption agencies would be wise to develop a range of adoption services for triad members, reflecting various placement options and the means for helping individuals to modify their choice, if necessary, to reflect changes in life circumstances and personal needs. This approach to adoption practice reflects an appreciation of the importance of developmental, contextual, and systemic influences on adoption triad members and moves us away from simplistic notions that any one type of adoption—whether confidential or fully disclosed—necessarily works best for everyone.

8

CLINICAL ISSUES AND TREATMENT STRATEGIES

The current mental health trend toward shorter treatments has led some clinicians to shorten or even eliminate the assessment process. This trend is unfortunate from our perspective, for an incomplete assessment is likely to lead to an inadequate understanding of the child's and/or family's problems, thereby potentially compromising the course of treatment. This problem is particularly true in the case of adopted children and their parents, who present with a number of unique individual and family circumstances that are often overlooked or misunderstood by treating therapists.

In moving from clinical assessment to treatment planning, the clinician must decide on the type of intervention that will most likely address the specific problems presented by the adopted child and his or her parents. In our opinion, no one treatment approach necessarily addresses the problems of adoptees better than others. What is more important than treatment modality or the therapist's theoretical orientation is a clear understanding of the adoption-related issues that are likely to emerge in the course of treatment and the availability of specific intervention strategies, incorporated into an overall treatment plan, that can help adoptees work through their unique life circumstances.

In this chapter we focus on three general issues:

1. areas of clinical assessment specific to adopted children and their parents;
2. common adoption themes that often are embedded in the symptom pattern of adopted children; and
3. clinical intervention strategies that specifically target adoption issues.

CLINICAL ASSESSMENT
ISSUES IN ADOPTION

Although not all clinical problems manifested by adopted children are directly connected to their adoptive family status, it is our experience and that of other clinicians in the adoption field (cf. Hartman & Laird, 1990; Reitz & Watson, 1992; Winkler et al. 1988) that the unusual life circumstances of these children and their parents often color individual and family dynamics, leading to specific symptom patterns. Consequently, exploring the role of adoption in the life of parents and children is a crucial part of the assessment process.

Interviewing Adoptive Parents

When interviewing adoptive parents prior to their child's treatment, there are five general areas related to adoption that need to be addressed:

1. motivation for adoption;
2. transition to adoptive parenthood;
3. attitudes about, and experience with, birth parents;
4. adoption revelation and the child's curiosity about his or her origins; and
5. the family's social support for adoption.

Information about these issues will help the clinician better understand the type of family and community context within which the child is being raised.

Parental Motivation for Adoption. An important, but often overlooked, area of inquiry concerns the role of children in adults' ideas about themselves as individuals and as a married couple (Reitz & Watson, 1992). For many adults, the capacity to have a biological child is at the core of their identity. Consequently, when faced with the reality of infertility, individuals typically experience a fundamental loss of a long-held image—for the woman, as capable of pregnancy and birth; for the man, as perpetuator of the family line (Blum, 1983; Schechter, 1970). The deep narcissistic wound of infertility can create great personal and interpersonal conflict, making it difficult for the couple to reach a mutual understanding of themselves as "infertile," let alone a mutual agreement about whether or not to pursue adoption. Because inadequate resolution of infertility issues can adversely affect the creation of a supportive postadoption child-rearing environment (Brodzinsky, 1997), it is important for clinicians to explore how parents have handled the stress and strain of infertility and whether the decision to pursue adoption was by mutual agreement or primarily a reflection of one parent's need.

It is sometimes believed that adjusting to infertility is a singular process of grieving the inability to conceive the long-desired biological child. As a result, clinicians often ignore the fact that adoptive parents frequently have experienced early pregnancy loss, which can complicate the grieving process, especially as the gestational age of the fetus increases (Goldbach, Dunn, Toedter, & Lasker, 1991). Exploring this aspect of loss with parents can help the clinician develop a richer understanding of the relationship between the adoptive parents' experience of infertility, the loss of biological children, their decision to pursue adoption, and their relationship with the child they have adopted.

Finally, some individuals and couples adopt for reasons other than infertility. In such cases, exploration of the motives underlying the decision to adopt often produces information that is critical for understanding family dynamics. For example, one of the authors recently worked with a couple who had chosen not to have their own biological children, but rather to adopt a child from a third-world country. A primary motive underlying their decision was the desire to "save" a child who might otherwise suffer a life of deprivation. Although viewing themselves as altruistic individuals, both parents expected their son, a 9-year-old boy from India, to feel grateful for having been adopted. This attitude, however, made it difficult for them to communicate comfortably with their son about his longing to know more about his birth mother and his sadness in being separated from her.

Transition to Adoptive Parenthood. Adoptive parents sometimes experience loss related to the adoption process that has occurred prior to the adoption of the child being presented for treatment. This type of loss can occur as a result of adoption disruption, when a previous child is either returned voluntarily to the agency by prospective adoptive parents prior to legal finalization, or the child is removed by the state because of concerns regarding the appropriateness of the placement. Another type of adoption-related loss occurs when a birth parent successfully contests the placement after it has occurred but before the adoption is finalized. Such losses can be devastating for the adoptive couple, undermining their confidence and sense of entitlement to a child and increasing their anxiety in relation to future adoption placements.

A second set of issues related to the transition to adoptive parenthood concerns the type of adoption chosen by parents, the reasons for their choice, their experience in the adoption process, and their expectations concerning their unique family circumstances. Because adoption is becoming increasingly varied and complex, clinicians must not assume that every family's motives, experiences, and expectations are similar. It is quite a different experience adopting a child of the same race from within one's own country as opposed to a child born in another country or of a different race. Similarly, adopting a healthy infant is quite different than adopting an older, special needs youngster. Exploring the reasons why parents have chosen a specific type of adoption can be useful in uncovering attitudes about race, ethnicity, and culture as well as parents' expectations concerning their ability to ameliorate the influence of prenatal difficulties and/or early social adversity experienced by so many special needs and foreign-born adopted children.

Another aspect of assessment usually involves discussions about the type of preparation for adoption that parents have received, either from agency personnel or through workshops. Individuals who adopt independently often receive little or no preparation for adoptive parenthood; those who adopt through agencies, on the other hand, often go through fairly extensive preplacement counseling and preparation. Such preparation, however, does not automatically equate with realistic expectations. In their longing for a child, many adoptive parents "screen out" the words of caution and thoughtful consideration voiced by adoption agency personnel. Too often, adoptive parents assume that with enough love—which they certainly believe they have at the time of placement—there are few, if any, problems that cannot be resolved. Sadly, by the time the family presents itself for assessment and treatment, this attitude may not only be shattered but replaced with anger, blame, despair, and helplessness.

Attitudes About and Contact With Birth Parents. Although the history of the adopted child begins in the birth family, the deep wish of the adoptive parents for the child to be "their own" and for their family to be an ordinary one, may lead to an underestimation of the importance of this part of their child's life, even in adoptions with some openness. As part of the assessment, clinicians need to explore the way in which the child's birth family and circumstances of the relinquishment are represented by adoptive parents (Brodzinsky & Brodzinsky, 1997). When birth parents are viewed in a positive, empathic, and respectful way by adoptive parents, it is usually easier for children to openly express curiosity about their origins in family discussions. Conversely, when the child's birth parents are devalued or demeaned by adoptive parents, children usually find it difficult to communicate their thoughts and feelings about their heritage. Orienting the adoptive parents to the profound importance of the birth family for the child will be an ongoing treatment goal for the therapist.

The clinician also needs to explore the amount of information that adoptive parents have about the birth family, the nature of information shared with the child, the reasons why certain information may have been withheld, and what type of contact, if any, the family has with birth parents. Although the trend today is for agencies to share a good deal of information about the birth family, even in confidential adoptions, there is still considerable variability among adoptive families in the amount and nature of information they possess. As we already have seen, some adoptions involve full disclosure between the adoptive and biological families as well as direct, ongoing contact over time; in other cases, especially in international adoption, virtually no information is known about the birth parents and no contact is possible. In the latter situation, parents often feel confused about how to handle the child's questions about his or her origins.

Although the degree of openness is a defining characteristic of the adoption, it must be remembered that in the early years of the child's life, the amount and nature of the contact between the families usually is evolving (Grotevant & McRoy, 1998). A thorough review of the history of involvement with the birth family, including the extent to which the child has been included in the contact and the reasons for any changes in the relationship between the families, will provide the clinician with a more comprehensive understanding of the kinship context within which the child is being raised.

Adoption Revelation and Children's Curiosity About Origins. One of the most difficult, but normative, tasks faced by adoptive parents is talking with their child about adoption (Brodzinsky et al., 1992). Parental anxiety is usually tied to their uncertainty about how the child will react to this information and whether parent-child ties will be weakened. Exploring the history and reactions in relation to adoption revelation provides the clinician with insight into adoptive parents' comfort with openness in communication and whether there has been any unusual adjustment problems regarding the child's awareness of his or her adoptive status. In addition, inquiring about the child's adoption story will offer the clinician an opportunity to reinforce the importance for the adoptive parents to think of their child as having a "whole life" that began, as all lives do, with a biological mother and father (Lifton, 1994; Nickman, 1985).

During this part of the assessment, the goal of the clinician is not only to learn the unique story of the child's adoption and what has been shared with, or withheld from, the child, but also to determine what parents believe their child understands about the information presented. Brodzinsky (1983) found that adoptive parents frequently overestimate the extent to which their children understand the information that has been shared. This pattern of misperception, coupled with the usual anxiety associated with adoption revelation, often leads parents to terminate prematurely the adoption disclosure process, which can place children at risk for unnecessary confusion and possible adjustment problems. Consider, for example, Joshua, a 9-year-old boy, who was interviewed by one of us.

> Prior to meeting with him, his mother took the interviewer aside and stated, "Joshua knows everything about his adoption. . . . We told him when he was five. . . . He asked a million questions and that was it." When seen individually, Joshua hesitated over the question, "Why do children need to be adopted?" and said that he did not want to answer it. However, toward the end of the interview, he asked to hear the question again. He then paused and, looking at the interviewer with great sadness, stated, "That is the master question of my life."

Joshua's story has been repeated to us hundreds of times in as many different ways. It represents what Lifton (1994) has called the "conspiracy of silence," wherein adoptive parents, adopted children, and birth parents are each wrapped in a veil of mystery, longing for things that cannot be shared with the other. It is critical for the clinician to understand how easily the child's connection to the birth family can be lost in the context of adoptive family life and how devastating that can be for some individuals.

Another issue in this area that needs to be explored is the adoptive parents' attitudes regarding their children's curiosity about their origins. Thoughts and fantasies about the birth family are extremely common, if not universal, among school-age adopted children (D. M. Brodzinsky, 1987, 1990). Adoptive parents, however, often have widely divergent reactions to their children's interests in their heritage. Some are very understanding and supportive of their child's "need to know." Others, however, are threatened by the child's curiosity, which can undermine a caregiving environment that is conducive to open adoption communication.

Social Support and Community Feedback About Adoption. Another area that requires assessment is the type of social and emotional support the family has received regarding adoption. This is especially true when parents pursue nontraditional adoption—that is, adoption across racial lines; adoption of older, special needs children; adoption of foreign-born youngsters; and adoption that includes some degree of openness. Lack of support from extended family and friends can undermine parents' confidence in their adoption decision and create unnecessary anxiety, not only in the preplacement period, but well after the adoption has been finalized.

It is also important to discuss with parents the type of feedback their children have received about adoption. In some cases, children are the objects of teasing and ridicule because they are adopted. This experience can be emotionally devastating for the child, accentuating feelings of being different, undermining self-esteem, and contributing to significant adjustment problems. Exploring whether parents are aware of such experiences in their child's life, and the way they have responded to them, adds yet another piece to the complexity of adoptive family dynamics.

Interviewing Adopted Children

Success in interviewing children about adoption issues is highly variable and dependent on the child's age, knowledge about adoption, and motivation to reveal deeply personal thoughts and feelings. Although some youngsters are very open about their adoption experiences from the very beginning of the assessment process, others require much more time and the establishment of a therapeutic alliance before such information is forthcoming. Some children, in fact, are never willing to discuss openly their adoption. For these youngsters, the clinician will need to explore their play themes and symbolic representations in drawings or stories in order to gain insight into the role of adoption in their individual and family dynamics.

In working with adopted children, four general assessment areas related to adoption are typically explored:

1. knowledge and feelings about adoption;
2. knowledge, attitudes, and feelings about the birth family;
3. family communication about adoption; and
4. feedback from others about adoption.

Knowledge and Feelings About Adoption. It is important to have a clear sense of what children understand about adoption, both generally and in relation to their own unique life circumstances. Because parents often misperceive their child's adoption knowledge and beliefs, the clinician cannot rely on the information provided by parents. Very often, children do not remember or have misunderstood adoption information previously presented by parents. In other cases, children know much more about their history than parents are aware.

Adoptive parents also commonly misperceive the complexity of children's feelings about being adopted. As youngsters enter the school-age years, a growing sense of ambivalence about their family status is often found (Smith & Brodzinsky, 1994, 1997). In many cases, parents are unaware of the confusion, sadness, and distress that children experience in this area of their life. Effective clinical work with adopted children will require that clinicians have a good understanding of what children know about adoption and how they feel about their unique family status.

Finally, children's feelings of connectedness to their adoptive family needs to be explored. Although parents may report a strong and secure bond between themselves and their children, the sense of attachment may not be reciprocated from the point of view of the child. This pattern may be especially true during developmental periods when children are struggling to understand and accept their dual connection to two families or when they have lived with the biological family or a previous foster family for some time, prior to adoption placement, and are experiencing a sense of divided loyalty.

Knowledge, Attitudes, and Feelings About the Birth Family. Children's knowledge, attitudes, and feelings about the birth family, including the circumstances surrounding the relinquishment, are directly connected to self-esteem issues. When the birth family has been represented by adoptive parents and others in sympathetic and empathic ways, children typically have an easier time incorporating this part of their history into a healthy sense of self. However, because many children come from backgrounds filled with social adversity (e.g., poverty, neglect, abandonment, abuse, parental psychopathology), they often receive, at the very least, mixed messages about their heritage.

When children do not ask many questions about their birth family, adoptive parents generally report that their children have little interest in this part of their life. We have found, however, that this conclusion is often inaccurate. In the majority of cases, children think and fantasize about birth family members much more than their parents realize. Exploring these thoughts and feelings with the child will facilitate a deeper understanding of the role adoption plays in the child's adjustment.

Finally, it is important to examine the type of contact, if any, that the child has with birth family members and whether he or she is satisfied with the contact. Most children are very curious about their heritage and want more information than they have been given. Some even want to search for their birth parents. Other children appear quite satisfied with the information they have and are not seeking to open up the adoption. Exploring this area with the child, including the underlying motives and expectations regarding birth family information and/or contact, will be useful in assessing the child's readiness for greater adoption openness.

Family Communication About Adoption. Adoptive parents and their children often have very different perspectives on the extent and ease with which the family discusses adoption-related issues. For example, parents may describe the family as being very open and comfortable about adoption issues, whereas children perceive their parents as uncomfortable, avoidant, and even threatened by this topic area. When children sense that parents are ambivalent about discussing adoption, it very often undermines their efforts to explore this aspect of their life. Assessing patterns and feelings about adoption communication not only will normalize and validate this process, but can be very helpful in facilitating greater openness between parents and children.

Adoption Feedback From Others. A final area that should be explored with children is the type of feedback they have received about adoption from others, especially peers. Too often, children receive negative messages about being adopted that are not shared with parents. For example, although they may be told by friends that "it's cool" to have two mothers and fathers, they also recognize that these same friends do not envy them for their adoptive status. In addition, some children are actually the object of ridicule and taunting by peers because they are adopted. Both experiences reinforce for the child the idea that adoption is not only "different" but deviant in the eyes of others; this perception can, in turn, undermine self-esteem. Finally, for interracial adoptees, the clinician needs to explore the extent to which children have experienced social discomfort and/or prejudice because of the physical differences between themselves and their parents. Too often, these experiences are not shared with adoptive parents and as a result become the basis for individual and family adjustment problems.

COMMON CLINICAL ISSUES IN ADOPTED CHILDREN

While growing up, adopted children are exposed to a variety of unique experiences that often create additional challenge or stress for these youngsters, both intrapersonally and interpersonally. In Chapter 3, we examined how many of these life experiences affect general as well as adoption-specific, family life cycle tasks. In this section, we describe how the complexities of adoption manifest themselves in terms of a number of clinical themes—separation and loss, relationship issues, and problems in self-development—which often are embedded in the symptom patterns of these individuals.

Separation and Loss

Adoption is inextricably linked to the experience of loss (Nickman, 1985). For later-placed children, the loss of family, or surrogate family, connections is overt, often acute, and sometimes traumatic. In contrast, for children placed as infants, loss is of necessity more covert, emerging slowly as the youngster begins to understand the magnitude of what has happened (D. M. Brodzinsky, 1987, 1990; Nickman, 1985). Adoptees not only lose their birth families and, in many cases, much-loved foster families, but also experience loss of social status associated with the stigma of being adopted. In addition, there may be loss of a clear sense of genealogical connections and, in the case of transracial and intercountry adoption, loss of cultural, ethnic, and racial ties. Children placed across racial lines also experience loss of privacy about their family status, which at times can be quite disconcerting. Consider for example, David, a 14-year-old Korean youngster, adopted at the age of 3 months. David lives with his white parents and two adopted siblings, both of whom are also white. In therapy with one of the authors, David reported the following:

> When I am by myself, or even with my friends, I don't think much about being adopted. When I go out with my parents and my brothers, it's different. I feel like I stand out, like everyone is looking at me. They know that I'm adopted. But they don't necessarily know that about my brothers because they look more like my parents. I don't like people knowing my business . . . about being adopted. But because I'm Korean and Mom and Dad aren't, then I can't stop them from knowing. I don't have any real privacy about my adoption.

Children's reactions to losses associated with adoption are highly variable (Smith & Brodzinsky, 1994, 1997). For some, the experience is minimal, with fleeting awareness of emotional pain and few, if any, long-term complications in adjustment. Others experience an intense and enduring feeling of deprivation and a pervasive sense of fragmentation and emptiness that can lead to significant long-term psychological difficulties (Lifton, 1994). For the majority of youngsters, however, adoption is experienced as only periodically stressful, with different types of adoption-related loss affecting the individual at different times. For example, sensitivity to birth parent loss, especially the loss of the birth mother, appears quite early in the dynamics of adopted children. Play themes representative of a missing or stolen mother are frequently noted by clinicians in children as young as 3 to 4 years of age, with more overt expressions of curiosity and concern about the birth mother usually observed by 5 to 7 years of age. Awareness of loss of genealogical connections as well as loss of identity, on the other hand, usually are not observed until at least adolescence (Grotevant, 1977).

We have argued elsewhere (D. M. Brodzinsky, 1987, 1990; Brodzinsky et al., 1992) that children's reactions to adoption-related loss, like their reaction to other forms of family disruption (e.g., death, divorce), are best understood within the context of a grief and bereavement model. Research and clinical experience indicates that children who experience various types of loss, like their adult counterparts, commonly display a host of emotional and behavioral reactions associated with grieving—confusion, anxiety, guilt, shame, anger, depression, acting out (Bowlby, 1980). Grieving is not ordinarily thought to be a pathological process; that is, individuals who are anxious, angry, and/or depressed over the death of a loved one usually are not identified as maladjusted. However, when grieving is impeded, because of intrapsychic conflicts and/or lack of support from others, it can lead to significant adjustment difficulties and even to serious forms of psychopathology (Bowlby, 1980). Brodzinsky (1990) has noted a number of factors that may impede an adjustment to the grief associated with adoption. To begin with, adoption is relatively rare—only 2% of children in the United States are adopted by nonrelatives—which increases the likelihood that the adoptee will feel that others, who do not share this life experience, will not understand what he or she is going through. In turn, this experience may foster feelings of "differentness" and undermine self-esteem and a sense of psychological well-being. A second complication is that the loss of the birth family, unlike the losses of signficant persons through death, is not necessarily permanent. As children come to understand that members of their birth family are alive and that reunions are possible, they may experience increased anxiety about being taken away from the adoptive family or, in some cases, anxiety associated with unrealistic fantasies of being rescued by the birth parents. These thoughts and feelings are, of course, complicated by the relationship— or lack of relationship—the children have had with the birth parents and their perception of the circumstances surrounding the relinquishment decision. When children are placed in infancy, they have no memory of the birth parents and may have little or no access to information about them. In these situations, what is lost is also unknown, which too often sets the stage for the development of distorted perceptions about one's background. As D. M. Brodzinsky

(1990) noted, the lost birth parents often linger as "ghosts" in the adoptee's mental and emotional life, which may interfere with a satisfactory resolution of the loss. In contrast, children placed at older ages often have very clear memories of their parents, which are likely to range across a spectrum of experience, from very nurturing interactions to memories of neglect, abuse, and various forms of parental dysfunction. These memories are likely to create confusion and ambivalence in older-placed adopted children, compromising their ability to resolve the grief they feel.

For some children, the knowledge that they were *voluntarily* placed for adoption often leads to feelings of being rejected or unwanted. In such cases, children may internalize responsibility for the relinquishment, believing that they were "given away" because of some characteristic that the birth parent found undesirable. In other cases, children may perceive their relinquishment as an *involuntary* removal from the birth family initiated by the state because of parental neglect, abuse, or incompetence, which in turn can compromise feelings of self-worth through the incorporation of negative parental characteristics. In still other cases, children may view the birth mother as an innocent victim whose child was taken from her. Fantasies of "undoing" the adoption and intense feelings of anger directed at the adoptive parents are common reactions in this situation. Consider the case of Wendy, a 7-year-old child adopted at birth.

> Wendy had always been an affectionate and reasonably compliant child. However, by the middle of her seventh year, she began asking a great many questions about her birth mother. Instead of being comforted by the answers her parents gave to the questions, she because increasingly agitated and angry. She demanded to see her birth mother and said that she was sure her birth mother must be very worried about her by now. "I know she is crying all the time. She doesn't know where her child is sleeping. I need to go there and tell her I am here. You are very bad to take a baby away and not even call and say the baby is sleeping and eating in a good home."

Finally, the sheer magnitude of loss associated with adoption, especially as it unfolds over time, can be quite difficult for the child to manage. When this loss goes unrecognized by society, which frequently is the case in infant placement, adoptees often experience a lack of emotional support from others as well as the absence of culturally sanctioned rituals that validate the reality and significance of what has occurred. These circumstances make it more difficult for adopted individuals to consciously acknowledge to themselves their sense of loss and find effective ways of coping with their sorrow.

Relationship Problems

The first developmental task faced by all children is the formation of a psychologically healthy attachment bond with a parent. Infant researchers have demonstrated that the child begins to seek a relationship with others a few hours after birth (Beebe & Lachman, 1988; Stern, 1985). When children are placed for adoption in early infancy, this crucial process appears to parallel the one found in nonadoptive families, leading ultimately to a reasonably secure parent-child bond by the end of the first year (Singer et al., 1985). In contrast, children placed beyond 6 months of age often show attachment-related difficulties (Yarrow & Goodwin, 1973; Yarrow et al., 1973) and in some cases may manifest Reactive Attachment Disorder (Hughes, 1997; Nadelman, in press). Some attachment-disordered children present as emotionally distant and unrelated, whereas others are overly friendly, dependent, and clingy. Consider, for example, the experience of Mrs. K, the adoptive mother of Susan, age 7, placed at 13 months of age, following physical abuse by the biological mother as well as three foster placements:

> Susan never seemed to warm up to us. From the very beginning she resisted being held and comforted. She would go stiff when we tried to cuddle with her . . . even now she doesn't come to us when she gets hurt. . . . I feel that the only time we exist for her is when she wants something . . . then she gets all friendly and sweet but we feel the falseness. Even after all this time, she doesn't feel that much for us . . . or really care about us.

In contrast, Mrs. P reported a different pattern of attachment-related problems in her 6-year-old boy, who was placed for adoption at 2 years of age, following multiple foster care placements.

> Eddie seemed to fit in right from the beginning. At first, we were delighted at how easy it was. He hugged and kissed us and called us Mommy and Daddy right away. But pretty soon we began to see that he was extremely anxious if we left him alone even to go into the next room. We also observed that he was overly friendly with strangers and wandered away from us in crowded places. As long as he was talking with someone, even a total stranger, he was unconcerned about where we were.

Attachment difficulties in adopted children can occur for many different reasons. In some cases, it may be associated with prenatal exposure to drugs or alcohol or result from neglect or abuse experienced in the biological family or a previous foster family. In other cases, attachment problems may be linked to the disruption associated with multiple residential moves prior to the adoptive placement. Parents adopting children from other countries also are finding an increased number of attachment-related problems in their children, especially in those youngsters who have lived for lengthy periods in institutional environments (Chisholm et al., 1995). Finally, attachment problems in adoptees can occur because of problems within the adoptive family. Typically, these problems occur either because of difficulties in the adoptive parents' attachment history and/or because of difficulties associated with unresolved issues associated with infertility. Adoptive parents may continue to harbor fantasies of their "perfect child" and still be grieving its loss. In such cases, adoption may be an act of reparation, with the child expected, at least unconsciously, to fulfill some expected role. Should the characteristics of the child, and/or the caregiving experience, not match parental expectations, it is likely to create frustration and disappointment on the part of adoptive parents and possibly undermine the parent-child bond.

   Another relationship issue that is often uncovered in the assessment and treatment of adopted children is divided loyalty (Butler, 1989). As children enter the elementary school years, they come to understand their dual connection to both the adoptive and birth families. However, the growing curiosity about their adoption and fantasies about their birth parents, although age appropriate (Rosenberg & Horner, 1991; Smith & Brodzinsky, 1994, 1997), may cause them to worry about their parents' reactions to the interest in their origins. This concern is especially true when children perceive their parents to be uneasy about birth family issues. For children placed at older ages, a sense of divided loyalty is even more common. In some cases, these children remain strongly bonded to birth family members or previous foster family members with whom they had lived for some time. In any event, older-placed children may resist becoming integrated into their adoptive homes because they believe that to do so means letting go of previously important relationships. Furthermore, if there is a lack of understanding by adoptive parents of the profound importance of these past relationships, the child is likely to experience considerable anger and to feel alienated in the new family. For these reasons, parents and mental health professionals must find ways of validating, and when appropriate, preserving the children's connections to the many caregivers and friends from the past.

Self-Development Issues

   The development of self in relation to others is one of the most crucial tasks of childhood. Stern (1985) suggests that this process begins at birth, with the young baby quickly becoming a vigorous seeker of social interaction and ultimately developing a sense of agency and self-awareness. Over time, the child's self-concept will develop in the context of mutual regulatory interactions with caregivers (Stern, 1985) and will come to mirror the perceptions and responses of others, especially parents, regarding the self. When parents are consciously or unconsciously disappointed. in the child, the quality of empathic response from the parent is likely to be compromised, undermining the child's self-esteem. Although this process occurs in all families, there are some unique circumstances in adoptive families that may create additional problems for the child's developing self system.

To begin with, adoptive parents must be able to put aside their longing for the desired biological child and emotionally invest in the children they have adopted. They must be able to see their children for who they are, not for who they want them to be, and respond in empathic and supportive ways. When this happens, adopted children are better able to accept themselves and enter into mutually satisfying relationships with family members. On the other hand, when the hopes and expectations of adoptive parents in relation to their children are not realized, the disappointment they experience may be reflected back to their children, undermining the latter's self-esteem. Unfortunately, we have witnessed this problem all too often in adoptive families, especially among middle- and upper-middle-class parents who place a high value on academic success, but who have adopted children who are struggling in school because of learning disabilities.

Self-esteem problems in adopted children also are tied to the way they view their birth parents and understand the circumstances of their relinquishment. When birth parents are viewed as uncaring, damaged, or unworthy individuals, and when children perceive the relinquishment as a rejection or abandonment, they are much more likely to internalize negative self-attributions and to experience embarrassment and shame regarding themselves and their adoption. Furthermore, because special needs adoptions often are connected to historical events (e.g., neglect, abuse, abandonment, parental psychopathology) about which adoptive parents may well have strong value conflicts, there is a greater likelihood that older-placed children will receive negative feedback from their parents about their origins and the circumstances of the relinquishment. It is exactly this type of experience that undermines self-acceptance among adopted children.

The development of a sense of agency and efficacy is viewed as fundamental to the child's emerging self system from widely divergent theoretical perspectives (Bandura, 1982; Stern, 1985). A purposeful self, capable of action and effective functioning, is believed to bolster positive self-esteem. Adopted individuals, however, have often been said to feel as if they do not have control over their own lives (Lifton, 1979, 1994; Sorosky et al., 1978; Winkler et al., 1988). Unlike their peers who have always lived with their biological family, adoptees have been "given up" by, or "taken" from, their birth family, cut off from much of the information about their origins, and typically prevented from gaining access to the information by adoption agencies, the court system, and sometimes by adoptive parents. As a result, they often feel as if they are not in charge of their lives, at least in the way they perceive others to be. In addition, they often feel as if the fundamental right to know about oneself—which is taken for granted by most people—has been denied, leading to a deep sense of frustration and helplessness.

A final clinical theme observed in adoptees, especially in the transition from adolescence to adulthood, relates to problems in the development and consolidation of identity (Grotevant, 1997; Lifton, 1994; Sorosky et al., 1975; Stein & Hoopes, 1985). Too often, adoptees have little information about their past and are prevented from gaining access to information that does exist. Cut off from their heritage and disconnected from their place within an intergenerational line, adoptees may experience a sense of alienation from both self and others—what Lifton (1994) has called "cosmic loneliness." This has been the experience of Beth, an 18-year-old adoptee, placed in early infancy.

> I often feel as if I don't really exist . . . I have no past . . . nothing that I can call my own . . . no sense of being a part of something. . . . I know that my family loves me and I feel the same way, but it still doesn't make a difference . . . I feel so alone. So alone.

Grotevant (1997) has noted that identity development is even more complicated for adoptees as additional dimensions of "differentness" are added to the family system. Thus, adoptees who are different from their parents in physical appearance, racial or ethnic background, personality characteristics, mental abilities, or talents often find it more difficult to fit comfortably into the family and to integrate their "differentness" into a secure sense of self. Finally, in special needs adoptions, children also have the additional challenge of integrating the reality of their birth family experiences, which may include neglect, abuse, and/or parental psychopathology, into a stable and consolidated identity. As we have already noted, the way adoptive parents portray the birth family and the circumstances of the relinquishment play an important role in determining whether the child's origins are internalized in a positive and ego-syntonic manner.

CLINICAL INTERVENTIONS
FOR ADOPTED CHILDREN

Although the problems presented by adopted children and their families are often amenable to traditional individual, family, and group therapy techniques, at times more structured interventions are necessary for uncovering and working through adoption-specific issues. Clinicians working in the field of adoption have found a number of strategies particularly useful in achieving this goal.

Lifebooks

Lifebooks are symbolic representations of a child's life. Typically constructed in the form of a loose-leaf binder, arranged chronologically, lifebooks include any information about the child's history deemed relevant to promoting greater self-knowledge and emotional well-being—from facts about the child's birthplace and information about birth family, including pictures and letters from birth parents, to information and materials representing previous foster care placements and the current adoptive family (Backhaus, 1984). Although adoption caseworkers often develop lifebooks for children in preparation for placing them in an adoptive home, the use of lifebooks as a clinical tool is more complicated. To begin with, lifebooks should be *constructed with the child* as part of individual or family sessions, not given to the child or adoptive parents as a completed product. Decisions about what is included in the lifebook are made in keeping with the child's age, readiness to deal with various issues, and availability of various information. When adoption issues are being explored and little factual information is available, children are encouraged to share their fantasies, hopes, and expectations about these issues and to incorporate this material into the lifebook, often in the form of drawings or some written expression. The clinical goal in using the lifebook is to facilitate children's thoughts and feelings about their heritage, the people they have lived with, the experiences they have had, and most important, about themselves. Lifebooks help to bring substance and order to the mystery and chaos experienced by adopted children—to give them a sense of where they have come from, where they are presently, and where they are going. As a clinical tool, lifebook work validates and normalizes children's curiosity about their origins; promotes a more realistic understanding of adoption, including the circumstances of the relinquishment; fosters a more positive view of the self; and, in the context of family sessions, opens up communication about adoption issues and strengthens connections between parents and children.

Pictorial Timelines

For adopted children who have experienced multiple residential moves, life often feels quite confusing. These youngsters have been exposed to so many caregivers, and have experienced so much disruption in their lives, that they cannot make sense of it. Sometimes just being able to bring order to this confusing history can be quite helpful to the child. In such cases, pictorial timelines can be very useful.

This technique involves helping children to represent, through drawings or paintings, the various people and places that have been part of their lives. To accomplish this task, the therapist needs to have a detailed placement history of the child. Children are first asked to draw what they remember (or imagine) about their birth family, followed by a similar drawing for each successive placement, ending with their current adoptive family. When children cannot remember where or with whom they lived, the therapist provides whatever information is available and encourages the youngster to incorporate it into the pictorial representation of that placement. Having produced a series of drawings, ordered along a timeline, children are able, with the help of the therapist, to begin making sense of the many abrupt changes they have experienced in their lives.

Therapeutic Rituals

Rituals are a common part of everyone's life. They are symbolic acts, co-constructed among the participants who take part in them, and are used for various purposes (Imber-Black, 1988). Among their various functions, rituals give special meaning to celebrations, life transitions, and membership within a group or community. They also are used for healing purposes as well as for the expression and containment of strong emotions. In addition, rituals allow for the incorporation of past traditions into current life circumstances and, as a result, foster feelings of being grounded or connected to something familiar or expected. Finally, rituals mark change and at the same time facilitate change. In this regard, they are very useful for therapeutic purposes.

The use of rituals in psychotherapy is now well established, especially among family systems theorists (Imber-Black, Roberts, & Whiting, 1988).

Only recently, however, have clinicians begun to use rituals in the treatment of adoptees and their families (Whiting, 1988).

In our own clinical work, we have used candlelighting ceremonies, planting of flowers and other vegetation, and picture taking as ways of celebrating aspects of adoption, strengthening adoptive family ties, remembering and validating the child's connection to his or her birth family, and helping the child cope with adoption-related loss. Regardless of the nature of the ritual, it must be conducted in a way in which its meaning is clearly understood by all family members, each of whom has an opportunity to share his or her thoughts and feelings during the ritual ceremony. Most important, rituals should be developed with the adopted child, not imposed on him or her.

Journal Writing and Written Role-Play Exercises

As adoptees move into adolescence, the ability to introspect increases. This developmental change opens up the possibility of using various forms of written expression to explore adoption issues. Teenagers who have some previous experience with diaries often find the assignment of keeping a journal to be quite natural and especially useful in exploring their thoughts and feelings about adoption. Whether or not the the journal material is shared in treatment sessions is, of course, the patient's decision. Because teenagers are particularly sensitive about privacy issues, the therapist can expect that much of the material may not be shared. Journal writing is beneficial, however, even when the patient decides not to share what has been written, if for no other reason that it tends to keep the individual focused on treatment issues between sessions.

Another intervention that we have found particularly useful in exploring adoption issues with older children and adolescents is a written role-play exercise. Here the adoptee is asked to write a letter to the birth parent, sharing whatever thoughts and feelings he or she wishes. After completing the letter, the patient is then asked to take the role of the birth parent who has received the letter and to write a letter in response, including anything he or she imagines the birth parent might choose to share. The patient then is asked to imagine receiving the birth parent's letter and to draft a response. This back and forth "correspondence with the self" continues for as long as the patient and therapist desire—sometimes through the bulk of the treatment process.

As an example, consider the following excerpts from Sara, a 17-year-old Korean adoptee, placed at 8 months of age.

Dear (blank),

   I feel hesitant writing to you because I don't know if you will want to get this letter. I don't even know whether you think about me, although I hope you do. Even though I don't know you and you really don't know me, you've been a part of my life since I was very little. I've often thought about who you are, what you look like, and what happened that made you give me up for adoption . . . that's been the hardest part, not knowing . . . it's what I need to find out.

Dear Sara,

   I received your letter today and was very surprised and very excited. I am so glad you wrote. In my heart you have never left me . . . I've kept you there. I don't want to upset your life with your family, but I would like to know about you . . . maybe see you sometime . . . write to me.

Several weeks later, Sara wrote the following response to her "birth mother."

I feel so funny thinking about the fact that you have thought of me all of these years, just like what I've been doing. There must have been times when we thought of each other almost at the same time . . . yet we don't know each other. Soon I will be 18 and I think I would like to meet you. Mom and Dad would help me. That's never been a problem. They know that I think about you a lot . . . talk to them about it sometimes. I only hope that I can find you . . . I will be thinking about you.

In the week that followed, Sara responded to herself:

When I received your letter it made me realize that you are older today than I was when you were born. We missed so much not being together. But I guess you have had a good life with your family. I also just thought that even if we meet, how can we talk to each other. You don't speak Korean and I don't speak English. That upsets me . . . not being able to understand you. . . .

As Sara's letters indicate, the written role-play exercise can be useful in uncovering the adoptee's hopes, expectations, and concerns about adoption issues. In these brief excerpts, Sara acknowledges her lifelong curiosity about her origins, the support she has received from her parents regarding adoption issues, her expectation that she would be well received by her birth mother, and her pain in realizing their inability to communicate because of a language barrier.

The Search Process

Much has been written about adoptees' search for their origins (Schechter & Bertocci, 1990). Although once thought to represent dissatisfaction with adoptive family life, and possible psychopathology in the adoptee, searching is now seen as a normal and, in some form, inevitable process among adopted individuals. Searching begins as an intrapsychic process in early childhood when adoptees begin to think about who their birth parents are and what happened that led to the adoptive placement. Soon, searching becomes an interpersonal process as children begin asking questions of their adoptive parents. For many adoptees, the search process goes no further. For others, however, searching continues as the individual seeks out additional information about his or her identity and heritage from the placing agency or attorney, or from other societal institutions. Finally, a smaller, but unknown, percentage of adoptees eventually decide to seek out birth family members. This process typically begins in adulthood and is usually focused on finding the birth mother (Schechter & Bertocci, 1990).

In working with adoptive families, a question that frequently arises is whether it is in the child's best interests to support a search process before he or she reaches adulthood—especially a process that would involve seeking new information and possibly contact with the birth family. Parents are often very anxious about this issue and seek the guidance of mental health professionals. Unfortunately, there is no research on searching by minors that would provide psychologists with guidelines for knowing when it is likely to be beneficial and when it may be detrimental to the child. Over the years, we have worked with many families who have decided to support their children's request to find out more about their birth heritage. At times, we have even suggested searching as a strategic clinical intervention to help family members overcome certain obstacles to therapeutic progress.

There are two basic types of searches that children and their families are likely to consider. The first involves a search for more information about the child's origins. Typically this process involves recontacting the adoption agency to obtain any information that is in their files—some of which may not have been shared at the time of placement and some of which may represent new information sent by the birth family after the placement. In other cases, the family decides to visit the child's place of birth, whether in this country or abroad. Pictures may be taken of the hospital, newborn nursery, and community within which the child was born. The child may be able to meet adoption agency personnel who were involved with the original placement. In cases of international adoption, families often visit the child's country of origin in order to help the youngster become more acquainted with his or her cultural, ethnic, and/or racial heritage. The second, and less common, type of search with minors involves an attempt to make contact with birth family members. Although adoption agencies are still reluctant to take part in this type of search, a growing number will consider assisting the family if they feel that family members have been adequately prepared and the child is ready, developmentally and emotionally, to cope with a reunion.

In making a clinical decision to support a search by a minor, the therapist should consider the following points. First, the decision to search should be based primarily on the child's need for, and readiness to accept, information and/or contact, not the parents' need. Second, searching should not begin until the child and parents have had an opportunity to explore together and separately their motivation for undertaking this process as well as their hopes, expectations, and fears about what is likely to happen. Gross misperceptions, unrealistic expectations, and undue fears need to be discussed and worked through before searching is initiated. Families need to recognize that their desire and need for contact may not necessarily be shared by birth family members. Third, therapists should ensure that the process proceeds slowly, making sure that the child and parents are coping well with the progress that has been made. In our experience, most children and teenagers in closed adoptions are satisfied with updated information and/or visits to their birth-place. Once achieved, these youngsters do not usually seek, and often resist, actual contact with the birth family, at least for the time being. Fourth, the therapist should ensure that the child is involved in the plans for searching. Although parents may make the initial contact with the adoption agency, children need to feel that they have some control over how the process is progressing. Fifth, when more detailed information about the birth family is obtained, it may become obvious that it would be inappropriate, given the child's age, to share the information or facilitate a reunion. Clinicians need to be prepared to assist the parents and child with this reality. Finally, clinicians need to recognize, and assist parents in recognizing, that the child's adjustment to new information, including contact with the birth family, is likely to proceed in an uneven fashion. At times, children will be at ease with the process and press forward with it; at other times, they may need to pull back from it to consolidate what has been experienced.

SUMMARY

Although adopted children seen in clinical settings present with a wide array of symptoms, a number of adoption themes are likely to emerge over the course of treatment. Many of these adoption issues are subtle and not readily expressed by children in therapy, regardless of the clinician's theoretical orientation. Therapists are urged to become more familiar with the unique clinical themes represented in the intrapsychic and interpersonal lives of adopted individuals and to begin expanding their repertoire of assessment and treatment techniques, including strategies that target adoption-specific issues.

9

CONCLUSIONS AND FUTURE DIRECTIONS

What can we conclude about adoption and its influence on children and their families? First, it is clear that adoption has become a very complex and highly varied form of family life. Compared with just a few decades ago, there is substantially greater diversity in the children being adopted as well as the individuals who are adopting them. This trend, which shows no evidence of reversing itself, limits our ability to make broad generalizations about outcomes for adopted children and their families. Second, it is equally clear that adoption is a highly successful societal solution for those children whose biological parents cannot or will not provide for them. There is no question that adopted children fare significantly better than those youngsters who are reared in institutional environments, in long-term foster care, or in neglectful or abusive homes. Third, although most adopted children adjust quite well to their new families, as a group, they are at greater risk than their nonadopted peers for a variety of academic and psychological problems, especially learning disabilities, attention deficits, and externalizing symptoms (e.g., aggression). Effect sizes for group differences are generally small, however. In addition, for children placed as infants, these problems are primarily found in middle childhood and early adolescence as opposed to other developmental periods. Fourth, although special needs adopted children often manifest multiple adjustment problems and are more likely to show postadoption difficulties than children placed as infants, these types of adoptions are generally successful. The key to success in special needs adoptions is good preplacement preparation of adoptive parents, realistic expectations on the part of these individuals, and a strong postadoption support network for the family. Fifth, children adopted across racial lines or from other countries also show remarkably successful integration into their new families, although questions regarding the development of positive racial identity among transracial adoptees remain unanswered. Sixth, there is a strong trend toward increasing openness in adoption today, which appears to be beneficial for both adoptive parents and birth parents, although its influence on children is still largely unknown. The few studies that have examined the adjustment of children in open adoption arrangements, however, do not support the grave concerns of critics who have argued that this type of placement is likely to undermine adoptive family relationships and the child's psychological well-being. Finally, from a clinical perspective, it is clear that adoption issues frequently are embedded in the individual and family dynamics manifested by adoptive family members seen in psychotherapy. Effective clinical work with this population requires that therapists, regardless of their theoretical orientation, incorporate adoption issues into both the assessment and treatment process.

As we approach the 21st century, it is natural not only to ask ourselves what we have learned about adoption from past research and clinical experience, but also to look ahead and consider where we should be going in this field. What type of research is needed to support the development of sound social policy, effective casework and clinical practice, and nurturing adoptive parenting? For us, a number of answers come to mind.

To begin with, adoption research must become more theory driven. For too long, research in this area has been primarily descriptive and atheoretical. Although typical of "early-stage" research in most areas of inquiry, this type of research limits our ability to understand the nature of the data being collected. As a research area matures, empirical studies must be developed within the context of well-articulated theoretical models. With respect to adoption, we are finally beginning to move in this direction, as reflected by the recent emergence of complex multidimensional models of adoption adjustment (Barth & Berry, 1988; Brodzinsky, 1990, 1993; Grotevant & McRoy, 1998; Groze, 1996; McRoy et al., 1988; Pinderhughes, 1996). Future research needs to continue in this regard. A related issue involves the type of questions that have informed adoption research. To date, most research has focused on relatively simplistic questions concerning rates of placement stability and whether adoptees are at greater risk for various types of adjustment problems than their nonadopted peers. Although these questions are important and have served a useful purpose in stimulating debate and empirical interest in this area, it is time to move on to more complex and relevant issues. If existing research tells us anything, it is that adoptees and their families manifest a high degree of variability in adjustment outcome. Some adopted children adjust very well; others show significant psychological problems. Thus, future research, whether on children placed as infants, special needs children, or transracial or intercountry adoptees, needs to focus more on individual difference factors that underlie the observed variability in adoption outcome. Particular attention needs to be paid to the influence of children's biological and prenatal histories, pre-placement rearing experiences, family transition experiences, and post-adoption developmental, family and social experiences on patterns of adjustment.

Like most areas in child development, adoption research has been primarily cross-sectional in nature. Consequently, we know very little about developmental processes in adoption adjustment. Although costly and logistically difficult to carry out, more longitudinal research on adoption needs to be conducted. Furthermore, because adoption is a lifelong issue (Brodzinsky et al., 1992; Reitz & Watson, 1992), this research needs to be extended beyond the childhood and adolescent years to examine the way in which adoption continues to influence adjustment patterns throughout adulthood.

Adoption research also needs to become more systems oriented. Although all children grow up within the context of multiple systems, for adoptees this process is simply more complex because of their dual connection to two kinship networks (Reitz & Watson, 1992) as well as those networks associated with previous foster families. Thus, attempting to examine the adjustment of adopted children in the context of only one of these networks, which has usually been the case in adoption research, is likely to produce a limited, and perhaps distorting, view of these youngsters. Adopting a more systemic, contextualistic perspective will certainly be a challenge for future researchers.

Another aspect of adoption that demands greater attention concerns the protective and ameliorative qualities of this form of family life. Adoption research has been too pathology oriented. It has focused primarily on the risks associated with this form of family life. Although important, this research trend has lost sight of the original goal of adoption—namely, to provide safe, permanent, and nurturing homes for children who cannot live with their biological families. Today, a growing number of children are entering foster care. Many of these youngsters have been prenatally exposed to drugs and alcohol; others have been subjected to parental neglect and/or abuse. Although these experiences were once thought to produce irreversible psychological damage in children, research (e.g., Barth & Needell, 1996) suggests that timely placement in a warm, stimulating, and nurturing home can offset some of the effects of early biological and social adversity. Because of the importance of these types of findings for child welfare policy and practice, we need much more research on the beneficial effects of adoption for children whose early life experiences place them at "high risk" for neurological, developmental, and psychological problems.

Greater sensitivity to racial, ethnic, and cultural differences also needs to be incorporated into adoption research. Most of what we know about issues in transracial placements is derived from studies examining African American children growing up in white families. Findings from these studies, however, may not generalize to the experiences of families characterized by other racial compositions. Furthermore, rather than focusing on whether transracial adoption either undermines or supports positive racial identity, it makes more sense to shift our attention to those adoptive family factors that are more or less supportive of healthy psychological adjustment and racial group identification in children placed across racial lines.

Perhaps no area in adoption is as controversial as the trend toward increased openness. Although much rhetoric has been generated by both proponents and critics of this practice, the debate has not been well informed by empirical data. As noted previously, we believe that most people have been asking the wrong question. Rather than focusing on whether open adoption is beneficial or harmful for members of the adoption triad, it makes more sense to us to explore the conditions under which greater or lesser amounts of openness are supportive of children's and parents' emotional well-being. What will be particularly challenging for researchers is exploring the *evolving* nature of relationships between the adoptive and biological families over the course of their respective life cycles. The work of Grotevant and McRoy (in press) represents an impressive step in the right direction.

Although this book has focused on the adjustment of adopted children and adoptive families, we would be remiss if we did not call attention to the need for additional research on birth parent adjustment. Less is known about postrelinquishment outcomes for birth parents than about the outcomes of other members of the adoption triad. Although existing research and clinical reports suggest substantial long-term problems for women who surrender a child for adoption (A. B. Brodzinsky, 1990, 1992), little data exist on those factors underlying the observed variability in birth parent adjustment. Furthermore, virtually nothing is known about postadoption outcomes of birth fathers or about the unique differences of child loss through adoption compared with child loss through induced abortion, miscarriage, stillbirth, or sudden infant death syndrome.

Finally, we would also like to see more interdisciplinary research on adoption. By its very nature, adoption has captured the interest of researchers and practitioners from a variety of scholarly and professional domains (e.g., social welfare, psychology, psychiatry, sociology, anthropology, medicine, nursing, law). Yet each of these groups has tended to focus on its own unique set of issues, without much regard for the perspective of other groups. The lack of interdisciplinary communication not only has limited our understanding of the complexities of adoption, but has impeded policy development as well as effective social casework and clinical practice. Building strong bridges between the various professional groups that affect policy and practice should be of the highest priority as we approach a new century and a new era for the field of adoption.

REFERENCES

Ainsworth, M. D. S., Blehar, M. C., Waters, E., & Wall, S. (1978). *Patterns of attachment: Psychological study of the Strange Situation.* Hillsdale, NJ.: Lawrence Erlbaum.

Andujo, E. (1988). Ethnic identity of transethnically adopted Hispanic adolescents. *Social Work, 33,* 531-535.

Association of Black Social Workers and Allied Professions (1983). *Black children in care: Evidence to the House of Commons Social Services Committee.* London: Author.

Bachrach, C. A. (1986). Adoption plans, adopted children, and adoptive mothers. *Journal of Marriage and the Family, 48,* 243-253.

Bachrach, C. A., Stolley, K. S., & London, K. A. (1992). Relinquishment of premarital births: Evidence from national survey data. *Family Planning Perspectives, 24,* 27-32, 48.

Backhaus, K. A. (1984). Life books: Tool for working with children in placement. *Social Work, 25,* 551-554.

Bagley, C. (1993). Chinese adoptees in Britain: A twenty-year follow-up of adjustment and social identity. *International Social Work, 36,* 143-157.

Bandura, A. (1982). Self-efficacy mechanisms in human agency. *American Psychologist, 37,* 122-147.

Baran, A., & Pannor, R. (1993). Perspectives on open adoption. *The Future of Children, 11,* 119-124.

Baran, A., Sorosky, A. D., & Pannor, R. (1974). Adoptive parents and the sealed records controversy. *Social Casework, 55,* 521-536.

Barth, R. P. (1987). Adolescent mothers' beliefs about open adoption. *Social Casework, 68,* 323-331.

Barth, R. P. (1988). Disruption in older child adoptions. *Public Welfare, 46,* 23-29.

Barth, R. P. (1993). Revisiting the issues: Adoption of drug-exposed children. *The Future of Children, 3,* 167-175.

Barth, R. P., & Berry, M. (1988). *Adoption and disruption: Rates, risks, and responses.* New York: Aldine De Gruyter.

Barth, R. P., & Brooks, D. (1997). A longitudinal study of family structure and size and adoption outcomes. *Adoption Quarterly, 1,* 29-56.

Barth, R. P., Courtney, M., Berrick, J., & Albert, V. (1994). *From child abuse to permanency planning: Pathways of children through child welfare services.* New York: Aldine de Gruyter.

Barth, R. P., & Needell, B. (1996). Outcomes for drug-exposed children four years post-adoption. *Children and Youth Services Review, 18,* 37-56.

Bartholet, E. (1993a). *Family bonds: Adoption and the politics of parenting.* Boston: Houghton Mifflin.

Bartholet, E. (1993b). International adoption: Current status and future prospects. *The Future of Children, 3,* 89-103.

Bausch, R. S., & Serpe, R. T. (1997). Negative outcomes of interethnic adoption of Mexican American children. *Social Work, 42,* 136-143.

Beebe, B., & Lachman, F. M. (1988). The contribution of mother-infant mutual influences to the origins of self- and object representations. *Psychoanalytic Psychology, 5,* 305-337.

Belbas, N. (1987). Staying in touch: Empathy in open adoptions. *Smith College Studies in Social Work, 57,* 184-198.

Benet, M. K. (1976). *The politics of adoption.* New York: Free Press.

Benson, P. L., Sharma, A. R., & Roehlkepartain, E. C. (1994). *Growing up adopted: A portrait of adolescents and their families.* Minneapolis: Search Institute.

Berry, M. (1989-1990). Stress and coping among older child adoptive families. *Social Work and Social Sciences Review, 1,* 71-93.

Berry, M. (1991). The practice of open adoption: Findings from a study of 1,396 families. *Children and Youth Services Review, 13,* 379-395.

Berry, M. (1993). Risks and benefits of open adoption. *The Future of Children, 11,* 125-138.

Bevan, C., & Pierce, W. (1994, November). Privacy, secrecy, and confidentiality in adoption. Paper presented at the Ethics in Adoption Conference, Minneapolis, MN.

Blakeslee, S. (1990). Parents' fear for future of infants born on drugs. *New York Times,* 1, 8-9.

Blum, H. P. (1983). Adoptive parents: Generative conflict and generational continuity. *Psychoanalytic Study of the Child, 38,* 141-163.

Bohman, M. (1970). *Adopted children and their families: A follow-up study of adopted children, their background environment, and adjustment.* Stockholm: Proprius.

Bohman, M. (1990). Outcome in adoption: Lessons from longitudinal studies. In D. Brodzinsky & M. Schechter (Eds.), *The psychology of adoption* (pp. 93-106). New York: Oxford University Press.

Bohman, M., & Sigvardsson, S. (1978). An 18-year prospective, longitudinal study of adopted boys. In E. J. Anthony, C. Koupernik, & C. Chiland (Eds.), *The child in his family: Vol 4. Vulnerable children.* New York: Wiley.

Bohman, M., & Sigvardsson, S. (1979). Long-term effects of early institutional care: A prospective longitudinal study. *Journal of Child Psychology and Psychiatry, 20,* 111-117.

Bohman, M., & Sigvardsson, S. (1980). A prospective, longitudinal study of children registered for adoption: A 15-year follow-up. *Acta Psychiatrica Scandinavica, 61,* 339-355.

Boneh, C. (1979). *Disruptions in adoptive placements: A research study.* Boston: Massachusetts Department of Public Welfare.

Bourguignon, J. P., Gerard, A., Alvarez Gonzalez, M. L., Fawe, L. & Franchimont, P. (1992). Effects of changes in nutritional conditions on timing of puberty: Clinical evidence from adopted children and experimental studies in the male rat. *Hormone Research, 38,* Supplement 1, 97-105.

Bowlby, J. (1969). *Attachment and loss. Vol. 1: Attachment.* New York: Basic Books.

Bowlby, J. (1973). *Attachment and loss. Vol. 2: Separation.* New York: Basic Books.

Bowlby, J. (1980). *Attachment and loss. Vol. 3: Loss.* New York: Basic Books.

Braungart-Rieker, J., Rende, R. D., Plomin, R., DeFries, J. C., & Fulker, D. W. (1995). Genetic mediation of longitudinal associations between family environment and childhood behavior problems. *Development and Psychopathology, 7,* 233-245.

Bretherton, I. (1987). New perspectives on attachment relations: Security, communication, and internal working models. In J. Osofsky (Ed.), *Handbook of infant development* (2nd ed.) (pp. 1061-1100). New York: Wiley.

Brinich, P. M. (1990). Adoption from the inside out: A psychoanalytic perspective. In D. Brodzinsky & M. Schechter (Eds.), *The psychology of adoption* (pp. 42-61). New York: Oxford University Press.

Brinich, P. M., & Brinich, E. B. (1982). Adoption and adaptation. *Journal of Nervous and Mental Disease, 170,* 489-493.

Brodzinsky, A. B. (1990). Surrendering an infant for adoption: The birth mother experience. In D. Brodzinsky & M. Schechter (Eds.), *The psychology of adoption* (pp. 295-315). New York: Oxford University Press.

Brodzinsky, A. B. (1992). *The relation of learned helplessness, social support and avoidance to grief and depression in women who have placed an infant for adoption.* Unpublished dissertation. New York University.

Brodzinsky, A., & Brodzinsky, D. (1997). Clinical assessment issues in the treatment of adopted children. *New Jersey Psychologist, 47,* 16-19.

Brodzinsky, D. M. (1983). *Adjustment factors in adoption* (Rep. No. MH34549). Washington, DC: National Institute of Mental Health.

Brodzinsky, D. M. (1984). New perspectives on adoption revelation. *Adoption and Fostering, 8,* 27-32.

Brodzinsky, D. M. (1987). Adjustment to adoption: A psychosocial perspective. *Clinical Psychology Review, 7,* 25-47.

Brodzinsky, D. M. (1990). A stress and coping model of adoption adjustment. In D. Brodzinsky & M. Schechter (Eds.), *The psychology of adoption* (pp. 3-24). New York: Oxford University Press.

Brodzinsky, D. M. (1993). Long-term outcome in adoption. *The Future of Children, 11,* 153-166.

Brodzinsky, D. M. (1997). Infertility and adoption adjustment: Considerations and clinical issues. In S. Lieblum (Ed.), *Infertility: Psychological issues and counseling strategies* (pp. 246-262). New York: Wiley.

Brodzinsky, D. M., & Brodzinsky, A. B. (1992). The impact of family structure on the adjustment of adopted children. *Child Welfare, 71,* 69-75.

Brodzinsky, D. M., Hitt, J. C., & Smith, D. W. (1993). Impact of parental separation and divorce on adopted and nonadopted children. *American Journal of Orthopsychiatry, 63,* 451-461.

Brodzinsky, D. M., & Huffman, L. (1988). Transition to adoptive parenthood. *Marriage and Family Review, 12,* 267-286.

Brodzinsky, D. M., Lang, R., & Smith, D. W. (1995). Parenting adopted children. In M. Bornstein (Ed.), *Handbook of parenting. Vol. 3: Status and social conditions of parenting* (pp. 209-232). Mahwah, NJ: Lawrence Erlbaum.

Brodzinsky, D. M., Radice, C., Huffman, L., & Merkler, K. (1987). Prevalence of clinically significant symptomatology in a nonclinical sample of adopted and nonadopted children. *Journal of Clinical Child Psychology, 16,* 350-356.

Brodzinsky, D. M., Schechter, D., Braff, A. M., & Singer, L. (1984). Psychological and academic adjustment in adopted children. *Journal of Consulting and Clinical Psychology, 52,* 582-590.

Brodzinsky, D. M., Schechter, D., & Brodzinsky, A. B. (1986). Children's knowledge of adoption: Developmental changes and implications for adjustment. In R. Ashmore & D. Brodzinsky (Eds.), *Thinking about the family: Views of parents and children.* Hillsdale, NJ: Lawrence Erlbaum.

Brodzinsky, D. M., & Schechter, M. D. (Eds.). (1990). *The psychology of adoption.* New York: Oxford University Press.

Brodzinsky, D. M., Schechter, M. D., & Henig, R. M. (1992). *Being adopted: The lifelong search for self.* New York: Doubleday.

Brodzinsky, D. M., Singer, L. M., & Braff, A. M. (1984). Children's understanding of adoption. *Child Development, 55,* 869-878.

Brodzinsky, D. M., & Steiger, C. (1991). Prevalence of adoptees among special education populations. *Journal of Learning Disabilities, 24,* 484-489.

Butler, I. C. (1989). Adopted children, adoptive families: Recognizing differences. In L. Combrinck- Graham (Ed.), *Children in family contexts* (pp 161-186). New York: Guilford Press.

Byrd, A. D. (1988). The case for confidential adoption. *Public Welfare, 46,* 20-23.

Cadoret, R. J. (1990). Biologic perspectives of adoptee adjustment. In D. Brodzinsky & M. Schechter (Eds.), *The psychology of adoption* (pp. 25-41). New York: Oxford University Press.

Cadoret, R. J., & Gath, A. (1980). Biological correlates of hyperactivity: Evidence for a genetic factor. In S. Sells, R. Crandall, M. Roff, et al. (Eds.), *Human functioning in longitudinal perspective.* Baltimore: William & Wilkins.

Cadoret, R. J., O'Gorman, T. W., Heywood, E., et al. (1985). Genetic and environmental factors in major depression. *Journal of Affective Disorders, 9,* 155-164.

Cadoret, R. J., Troughton, E., O'Gorman, T. W., et al. (1986). An adoption study of genetic and environmental factors in drug abuse. *Archives of General Psychiatry, 43,* 1131-1136.

Carey, W. B., Lipton, W. L., & Myers, R. A. (1974). Temperament in adopted and foster babies. *Child Welfare, 53,* 352-359.

Carter, E. A., & McGoldrick, M. (Eds.). (1980). *The family life cycle.* New York: Gardner Press.

Chapman, D., Dorner, P., Silber, K., & Winterberg, T. (1986). Meeting the needs of the adoption triangle through open adoption: The birthmother. *Child and Adolescent Social Work, 3,* 203-213.

Chapman, D., Dorner, P., Silber, K., & Winterberg, T. (1987a). Meeting the needs of the adoption triangle through open adoption: The adoptive parent. *Child and Adolescent Social Work, 4,* 3-12.

Chapman, D., Dorner, P., Silber, K., & Winterberg, T. (1987b). Meeting the needs of the adoption triangle through open adoption: The adoptee. *Child and Adolescent Social Work, 4,* 78-91.

Charles, R., Rashid, S., & Thoburn, J. (1992). The placement of black children with permanent new families. *Adoption and Fostering, 16,* 13-19.

Chestang, L. (1972). The dilemma of bi-racial adoption. *Social Work, 17,* 100-105.

Chimezie, A. (1975). Transracial adoption of black children. *Social Work, 20,* 296-301.

Chisolm, K., Carter, M., Ames, E. W., & Morison, S. J. (1995). Attachment security and indiscriminately friendly behavior in children adopted from Romanian orphanages. *Development and Psychopathology, 7,* 283-294.

Christian, C. L., McRoy, R. G., Grotevant, H. D., & Bryant, C. (In press). Grief resolution of birthmothers in confidential, time-limited mediated, ongoing mediated, and fully disclosed adoptions. *Adoption Quarterly.*

Cicchetti, D., Toth, S. L., & Lynch, M. (1995). Bowlby's dream comes full circle: The application of attachment theory to risk and psychopathology. In T. Ollendick & R. Prinz (Eds.), *Advances in Clinical Child Psychology: Vol. 17* (pp. 1-75). New York: Plenum.

Cocozzelli, C. (1989). Predicting the decision of biological mothers to retain or relinquish their babies for adoption: Implication for open placement. *Child Welfare, 68,* 33-44.

Cohen, J. S., & Westhues, A. (1995). A comparison of self-esteem, school achievement, and friends between intercountry adoptees and their siblings. *Early Child Development and Care, 106* 205-224.

Cole, E. S. (1985). Adoption: History, policy, and program. In J. Laird & A. Hartman (Eds.), *A handbook of child welfare.* New York: Free Press.

Cole, E. S., & Donley, K. S. (1990). History, values, and placement policy issues in adoption. In D. Brodzinsky & M. Schechter (Eds.), *The psychology of adoption* (pp. 273-294). New York: Oxford University Press.

Coon, H., Carey, G., Corley, R., & Fulker, D. (1992). Identifying children in the Colorado Adoption Project at risk for conduct disorder. *Journal of the American Academy of Child and Adolescent Psychiatry, 31,* 503-511.

Coon, H., Carey, G., Fulker, D. W., & DeFries, J. C. (1993). Influences of school environment on the academic achievement scores of adopted and nonadopted children. *Intelligence, 17,* 70-104.

Crittenden, P. M. (1988). Relationships at risk. In J. Belsky & T. Nezworski (Eds.), *Clinical implications of attachment theory* (pp. 136-174). Hillsdale, NJ: Lawrence Erlbaum.

Dalen, M., & Saetersdal, B. (1987). *Intercountry adopted children in Norway: Socio-cultural factors, identity, and adjustment.* Oslo: Norwegian Institute of Special Education.

Daly, K. (1988). Reshaped parenthood identity: The transition to adoptive parenthood. *Journal of Contemporary Ethnography, 17,* 40-66.

Daly, K. (1989, October). Infertility resolution and adoption readiness. *Families in Society: The Journal of Contemporary Human Services, 71,* 483-492.

DeBerry, K. M., Scarr, S., & Weinberg, R. (1996). Family racial socialization and ecological competence: Longitudinal assessments of African-American transracial adoptees. *Child Development, 67,* 2375-2399.

Deutsch, D. K., Swanson, J. M., Bruell, J. H., Cantwell, D. P., Weinberg, F., & Baren, M. (1982). Overrepresentation of adoptees in childen with the attention deficit disorder. *Behavior Genetics, 12,* 231-238.

Deutsch, H. (1945). *The psychology of women: A psychoanalytic interpretation (Vol. 2).* New York: Grune and Stratton.

DeVoid, D. E., Pineiro-Carrerro, V. M., Goodman, Z., & Latimer, J. S. (1992). Chronic active hepatitis B infection in Romanian adoptees. *Journal of Pediatric and Gastroenterological Nutrition, 19,* 431-436.

Dickson, L. R., Heffron, W. M., & Parker, C. (1990). Children from disrupted and adoptive homes on an inpatient unit. *American Journal of Orthopsychiatry, 60,* 594-602.

Elbow, M. (1986). From caregiving to parenting: Family formation with adopted older children. *Child Welfare, 31,* 366-370.

Epstein, Y. M., & Rosenberg, H. S. (1997). He does, she doesn't; she does, he doesn't: Couple conflicts about infertility. In S. Lieblum (Ed.), *Infertility: Psychological issues and counseling strategies* (pp. 129-148). New York: Wiley.

Etter, J. (1993). Levels of cooperation and satisfaction in 56 open adoptions. *Child Welfare, 72,* 257-267.

Everett, R., & Schecter, M. D. (1971). A comparative study of prenatal anxiety in the unwed mother. *Child Psychiatry and Human Development, 2,* 84-91.

Fahlberg, V. (1979). *Attachment and separation.* Michigan Department of Social Services.

Fanshel, D. (1972). *Far from the reservation.* Metuchen, NJ: Scarecrow Press.

Fanshel, D., & Shinn, E. B. (1978). *Children in foster care.* New York: Columbia University Press.

122 CHILDREN'S ADJUSTMENT TO ADOPTION

Feigelman, W., & Silverman, A. R. (1983). *Chosen children: New patterns of adoptive relationships*. New York: Praeger.

Fergusson, D. M., Lynskey, M., & Horwood, L. J. (1995). The adolescent outcomes of adoption: A 16-year longitudinal study. *Journal of Child Psychiatry and Psychiatry, 36,* 597-615.

Festinger, T. (1986). *Necessary risk: A study of adoptions and disrupted adoptive placements.* Washington, DC: Child Welfare League of America.

Festinger, T. (1990). Adoption disruption: Rates and correlates. In D. Brodzinsky & M. Schechter (Eds.), *The psychology of adoption* (pp. 201-220). New York: Oxford University Press.

Fisher, L., Ames, E. W., Chisolm, K., & Savoie, L. (1997). Problems reported by parents of Romanian orphans adopted to British Columbia. *International Journal of Behavioral Development, 20,* 67-82.

Fullerton, C. S., Goodrich, W., & Berman, L. B. (1986). Adoption predicts psychiatric treatment resistances in hospitalized adolescents. *Journal of the American Academy of Child Psychiatry, 25,* 542-551.

Gershenson, C. P. (1984). The twenty-year trend of federally assisted foster care. *Child Welfare Research Notes #8.* Washington, DC: Administration for Children, Youth, and Families: Department of Health and Human Services.

Glidden, L. M. (1991). Adopted children with developmental disabilities. Post-adoptive family functioning. *Children and Youth Services Review, 13,* 363-378.

Goldbach, K. R. C., Dunn, D. S., Toedter, L. J., & Lasker, J. N. (1991). The effects of gestational age and gender on grief after pregnancy loss. *American Journal of Orthopsychiatry, 61,* 461-467.

Goldberg, D., & Wolkind, S. N. (1992). Patterns of psychiatric disorder in adopted girls: A research note. *Journal of Child Psychology and Psychiatry, 33,* 935-940.

Goldfarb, W. (1945). Psychological privation in infancy and psychological adjustment. *American Journal of Orthopsychiatry, 15,* 247-255.

Griffith, D. R., Azuma, S. D., & Chasnoff, I. J. (1994). Three-year outcome of children exposed prenatally to drugs. *Journal of the American Academy of Child and Adolescent Psychiatry, 33,* 20-27.

Gross, H. E. (1993). Open adoption: A research-based literature review and new data. *Child Welfare, 77,* 269-284.

Grotevant, H. D. (1997). Coming to terms with adoption: The construction of identity from adolescence into adulthood. *Adoption Quarterly, 1,* 3-27.

Grotevant, H. D., & McRoy, R. G. (1998). *Openness in adoption: Exploring family connections.* New York: Sage.

Grotevant, H. D., McRoy, R. G., Elde, C. L., & Fravel, D. L. (1994). Adoptive family system dynamics: Variations by level of openness in adoption. *Family Process, 33,* 125-146.

Grotevant, H. D., Scarr, S., & Weinberg, R. A. (1977). Patterns of interest similarity in adoptive and biological families. *Journal of Personality and Social Psychology, 35,* 667-676.

Grow, L. J., & Shapiro, D. (1974). *Black children—white parents.* New York: Child Welfare League of America.

Groze, V. (1986). Special-needs adoptions. *Children and Youth Services Review, 8,* 363-373.

Groze, V. (1996). *Successful adoptive families: A longitudinal study of special needs adoption.* Westport, CT: Praeger.

Groze, V., & Ileana, D. (1996). A follow-up study of adopted children from Romania. *Child and Adolescent Social Work, 13,* 541-565.

Gyorkos, T. W., & MacLean, J. D. (1992). Medical evaluation of children adopted from abroad. *Journal of the American Medical Association, 268,* 410.

Hajal, F., & Rosenberg, E. G. (1991). The family life cycle in adoptive families. *American Journal of Orthopsychiatry, 61,* 78-85.

Hartman, A., & Laird, J. (1990). Family treatment after adoption: Common themes. In D. Brodzinsky & M. Schechter (Eds), *The psychology of adoption* (pp. 221-239). New York: Oxford University Press.

Haugaard, J. J. (In press). Is adoption a risk factor for the development of adjustment problems? *Clinical Psychology Review.*

Hayes, P. (1993). Transracial adoption: Politics and ideology. Child Welfare, *52,* 301-310.

Holden, N. I. (1991). Adoption and eating disorders. A high-risk group? *British Journal of Psychiatry, 158,* 829-833.

Hoopes, J. L. (1982). *Prediction in child development: A longitudinal study of adoptive and nonadoptive families.* New York: Child Welfare League of America.

Hoopes, J. L. (1990). Adoption and identity formation. In D. Brodzinsky & M. Schechter (Eds.), *The psychology of adoption* (pp. 144-166). New York: Oxford University Press.

Horn, J. M. (1983). The Texas adoption project: Adopted children and their intellectual resemblance to biological and adoptive parents. *Child Development, 54,* 268-275.

Horn, J. M., Green, M., Carney, R., & Erickson, M. (1975). Bias against genetic hypotheses in adoption studies. *Archives of General Psychiatry, 32,* 1365-1367.

Hostetter, M. K., Iverson, S., Thomas, W., McKensie, D., Dole, K., & Johnson, D. E. (1991). Medical evaluation of internationally adopted children. *New England Journal of Medicine, 325,* 479-485.

Huffman, L., & Brodzinsky, D. M. (1997). Predictors of adjustment in preschool adopted children. Unpublished manuscript.

Hughes, D. (1997). *Facilitating developmental attachment.* Northvale, NJ: Jason Aronson.

Imber-Black, E. (1988). Ritual themes in families and family therapy. In E. Imber-Black, J. Roberts, & R. Whiting (Eds.), *Rituals in families and family therapy* (pp. 47-83). New York: Norton.

Imber-Black, E., Roberts, J., & Whiting, R. (Eds.). (1988). *Rituals in families and family therapy.* New York: Norton.

Johnson, A., & Groze, V. (1993). The orphaned and institutionalized children of Romania. *Journal of Emotional and Behavioral Problems, 2,* 49-52.

Johnson, D. E., Miller, L. C., Iverson, S., Thomas, W., Franchino, W., Dole, K., Kiernan, M. T., Georgieff, M. K., & Hostetter, M. K. (1992). The health of children adopted from Romania. *Journal of the American Medical Association, 268,* 3446-3451.

Johnson, F., & Fein, E. (1991). The concept of attachment: Applications to adoption. *Child and Youth Services Review, 13,* 397-412.

Kadushin, A. (1980). *Child welfare services* (3rd edition). New York: Macmillan.

Kadushin, A., & Martin, J. (1988). *Child welfare services* (4th ed.). New York: Macmillan.

Kagan, R. M., & Reid, W. J. (1986). Critical factors in the adoption of emotionally disturbed youth. *Child Welfare, 65,* 63-74.

Katz, L. (1986). Parental stress factors for success in older child adoption. *Child Welfare, 65,* 569-578.

Kaye, K. (1990). Acknowledgment or rejection of differences? In D. Brodzinsky & M. Schechter (Eds.), *The psychology of adoption* (pp. 121-143). New York: Oxford University Press.

Kim, W. J. (1995). International adoption: A case review of Korean children. *Child Psychiatry and Human Development, 25,* 141-154.

Kim, W. J., Davenport, C., Joseph, J., Zrull, J., & Woolford, E. (1988). Psychiatric disorder and juvenile delinquency in adopted children and adolescents. *Journal of the American Academy of Child and Adolescent Psychiatry, 27,* 111-115.

Kirk, H. D. (1964). *Shared fate.* New York: Free Press.

Kirk, H. D. (1981). *Adoptive kinship—A modern institution in need of reform.* Toronto: Butterworth.

Kojis, J. (1990). *Psychologists' attitudes toward adopted children.* Unpublished dissertation, The Fielding Institute, Santa Barbara, CA.

Kopp, C. B. (1983). Risk factors in development. In P. Mussen (Ed.), *Handbook of child psychology: Vol 2. Infancy and developmental psychology.* New York: Wiley.

Kotsopoulos, S., Cote, A., Joseph, L., Pentland, N., Chryssoula, S., Sheahan, P., & Oke, L. (1988). Psychiatric disorders in adopted children. *American Journal of Orthopsychiatry, 58,* 608-612.

Kotsopoulos, S., Walker, S., Copping, W., Cote, A., & Stavrakaki, C. (1993). A psychiatric follow-up study of adoptees. *Canadian Journal of Psychiatry, 38,* 391-396.

Kraft, A., Palombo, J., Mitchell, D., Woods, P., & Schmidt, A. (1985a). Some theoretical considerations on confidential adoptions. Part 1: The birth mother. *Child and Adolescent Social Work, 2,* 13-21.

Kraft, A., Palombo, J., Mitchell, D., Woods, P., & Schmidt, A. (1985b). Some theoretical considerations on confidential adoptions. Part 2: The adoptive parent. *Child and Adolescent Social Work, 2,* 69-82.

Kraft, A., Palombo, J., Woods, P., Schmidt, A., & Tucker, N. (1985). Some theoretical considerations on confidential adoptions. Part 3: The adopted child. *Child and Adolescent Social Work, 2,* 139-153.

Kraus, J. (1978). Family structure as a factor in the adjustment of adopted children. *British Journal of Social Work, 8,* 327-337.

Lamb, M. (Ed.). (1982). *Nontraditional families: Parenting and child development.* Hillsdale, NJ: Lawrence Erlbaum.

Lambert, L., & Streather, J. (1980). *Children in changing families: A study of adoption and illegitimacy.* London: MacMillan.

Lazarus, R. S. (1991). *Emotion and adaptation.* New York: Oxford University Press.

Lazarus, R. S., & Folkman, S. (1984). *Stress, appraisal, and coping.* New York: Springer.

Levine, C., & Stein, G. L. (1994). *Orphans of the HIV epidemic: Unmet need in six U.S. cities.* New York: The Orphan Project.

Levitsky, D. A., & Strupp, B. J. (1995). Malnutrition and the brain: Changing concepts, changing concerns. *Journal of Nutrition, 125,* 2212-2220.

Levy-Shiff, R., Bar, O., & Har-Even, D. (1990). Psychological adjustment of adoptive parents-to-be. *American Journal of Orthopsychiatry, 60,* 258-267.

Lieblum, S. R., & Greenfield, D. A. (1997). The course of infertility: Immediate and long-term reactions. In S. Lieblum (Ed.), *Infertility: Psychological issues and counseling strategies* (pp. 83-102). New York: Wiley.

Lifton, B. J. (1979). *Lost and found: The adoption experience.* New York: Dial Press.

Lifton, B. J. (1994). *Journey of the adopted self: A quest for wholeness.* New York: Basic Books.

Lindholm, B. W., & Touliatos, J. (1980). Psychological adjustment of adopted and nonadopted children. *Psychological Reports, 46,* 307-310.

Lipman, E. L., Offord, D. R., Racine, Y. A., & Boyle, M. H. (1992). Psychiatric disorders in adopted children: A profile from the Ontario Child Health Study. *Canadian Journal of Psychiatry, 37,* 627-633.

Loehlin, J. C., Willerman, L., and Horn, J. M. (1985). Personality resemblances in adoptive families when the children are late-adolescent or adult. *Journal of Personality and Social Psychology, 48,* 376-392.

Main, M., & Goldwyn, R. (1984). Predicting rejecting of her infant from mother's representation of her own experience: Implications for the abused-abusing intergenerational cycle. *Child Abuse and Neglect, 8,* 203-217.

Main, M., Kaplan, N., & Cassidy, J. C. (1985). Security in infancy, childhood and adulthood: A move to the level of representation. *Monographs of the Society for Research in Child Development, 50,* (1-2. Serial No. 209), 66-104.

Marcovitch, S., Cesaroni, L., Roberts, W., & Swanson, C. (1995). Romanian adoption: Parents' dreams, nightmares, and realities. *Child Welfare, 74,* 993-1017.

Marshall, M. J., Marshall, S., & Heer, M. J. (1994). Characteristics of abstinent substance abusers who first sought treatment in adolescence. *Journal of Drug Education, 24,* 151-162.

Maugharn, B., & Pickles, A. (1990). Adopted and illegitimate children growing up. In L. Robins & M. Rutter (Eds.), *Straight and devious pathways from childhood to adulthood* (pp. 36-61). New York: Cambridge University Press.

Maza, P. (1983). Characteristics of children free for adoption. *Child Welfare Research Notes #2.* Washington, DC: Administration for Children, Youth, and Families: Department of Health and Human Services.

McDermott, M. T. (1993). The case of independent adoption. *The Future of Children, 11,* 146-152.

McEwan, K. L., Costello, C. G., & Taylor, P. J. (1987). Adjustment to infertility. *Journal of Abnormal Psychology, 96,* 108-116.

McRoy, R. G., & Grotevant, H. D. (1988). Open adoptions: Practice and policy issues. *Journal of Social Work and Human Sexuality, 6,* 119-132.

McRoy, R. G., Grotevant, H. D., & Zurcher, L. A. (1988). *The development of emotional disturbance in adopted adolescents.* New York: Praeger.

McRoy, R. G., Oglesby, Z., & Grape, H. (1997). Achieving same-race adoptive placements for African American children: Culturally sensitive practice approaches. *Child Welfare, 76,* 85-104.

McRoy, R. G., & Zurcher, L. A. (1983). *Transracial and inracial adoptees.* Springfield, IL: Thomas.

McRoy, R. G., Zurcher, L. A., Lauderdale, M. L., & Anderson, R. N. (1982). Self esteem and racial identity in transracial and inracial adoptees. *Social Work, 27,* 522-526.

Meezan, W., & Shireman, J. F. (1985). *Care and commitment: Foster parent adoption decisions.* New York: State University of New York Press.

Melina, L. R., & Roszia, S. K. (1993). *The open adoption experience.* New York: HarperCollins.

Mendenhall, T. J., Grotevant, H. D., & McRoy, R. G. (1996). Adoptive couples: Communication and changes made in openness levels. *Family Relations, 45,* 223-229.

Menlove, F. L. (1965). Aggressive symptoms in emotionally disturbed adopted children. *Child Development, 36,* 519-532.

Miall, C. (1987). The stigma of adoptive parent status: Perceptions of community attitudes toward adoption and the experience of informal social sanctioning. *Journal of Applied Family and Child Studies, 36,* 34-39.

Mikawa, J. K., & Boston, J. A. (1968). Psychological characteristics of adopted children. *Psychiatry Quarterly Supplement, 42,* 274-281.

Miller, L. C., Kiernan, M. T., Mathers, M. I., & Klein-Gitelman, M. (1995). Developmental and nutritional status of internationally adopted children. *Archives of Pediatric and Adolescent Medicine, 149,* 40-44.

Moore, R., & Camarda, T. (1993). Drug-exposed children: Fresh reasons for concern. *Leake and Watts Newsletter, 4,* 1-4.

Morison, S. J., Ames, E. W., & Chisolm, K. (1995). The development of children adopted from Romanian orphanages. *Merrill-Palmer Quarterly, 41,* 411-430.

Mosher, W. D., & Pratt, W. F. (1991). Fecundity and infertility in the United States: Incidence and trend. *Fertility and Sterility, 56,* 192-193.

Nadelman, A. (1997). Assessment and treatment of attachment-impaired adopted children. *New Jersey Psychologist, 47,* 27-29.

National Committee for Adoption. (1989). *Adoption Factbook.* Washington, DC: National Committee for Adoption.

Nelson, K. (1985). *On the frontier of adoption: A study of special needs adoptive families.* New York: Child Welfare League of America.

Newman, J. L., Roberts, L. R., & Syre, C. R. (1993). Concepts of family among children and adolescents: Effects of cognitive level, gender, and family structure. *Developmental Psychology, 29,* 951-962.

Nickman, S. L. (1985). Losses in adoption: The need for dialogue. *Psychoanalytic Study of the Child, 40,* 365-398.

Norvell, M., & Guy, R. F. (1977). A comparison of self-concept in adopted and nonadopted adolescents. *Adolescence, 12,* 443-448.

Okun, B. (1996). *Understanding diverse families: What practitioners need to know.* New York: Guilford.

Pannor, R., & Baran, A. (1984). Open adoption as standard practice. *Child Welfare, 63,* 245-250.

Pannor, R., Sorosky, A. D., & Baran, A. (1974). Opening the sealed record in adoption: The human need for continuity. *Journal of Jewish Communal Service, 51,* 188-196.

Partridge, S., Hornby, H., & McDonald, T. (1986). *Legacies of loss—visions of gain: An inside look at adoption disruption.* Portland, ME: University of Southern Maine Press.

Piersma, H. L. (1987). Adopted children and inpatient psychiatric treatment: A retrospective study. *The Psychiatric Hospital, 18,* 153-158.

Pinderhughes, E. E. (1996). Toward understanding family readjustment following older child adoptions: The interplay between theory generation and empirical research. *Children and Youth Services Review, 18,* 115-138.

Pinderhughes, E. E., Leddick, C., Nix, R., & Smith, M. T. (1995, April). Family readjustment following older child adoptions: The role of cognitions. Paper presented at the biennial meeting of the Society for Research in Child Development, Indianapolis, IN.

Plomin, R., & DeFries, J. (1985). *Origins of individual differences in infancy: The Colorado Adoption Project.* Orlando, FL: Academic Press.

Reitz, M., & Watson, K. W. (1992). *Adoption and the family system.* New York: Guilford.

Rogeness, G. A., Hoppe, S. K., Macedo, C. A., Fischer, C., & Harris, W. R. (1988). Psychopathology in hospitalized adopted children. *Journal of the American Academy of Child and Adolescent Psychiatry, 27,* 628-631.

Rosenberg, E. B., & Horner, T. M. (1991). Birth parent romances and identity formation in adopted children. *American Journal of Orthopsychiatry, 61,* 70-77.

Rosenthal, J. A. (1993). Outcomes of adoption of children with special needs. *The Future of Children, 3,* 77-88.

Rosenthal, J. A., & Groze, V. (1992). *Special needs adoption: A study of intact families.* New York: Praeger.

Rosenthal, J. A., Schmidt, D., & Conner, J. (1988). Predictors of special needs adoption disruption: An exploratory study. *Children and Youth Services Review, 10,* 101-117.

Rushton, A., & Minnis, H. (1997). Transracial family placements. *Journal of Child Psychology and Psychiatry, 38,* 147-159.

Sack, W. H., & Dale, D. (1982). Abuse and deprivation in failing adoptions. *Child Abuse and Neglect, 6,* 443-451.

Scarr, S., & Weinberg, R. A. (1976). IQ test performance of black children adopted by white families. *American Psychologist, 31,* 726-739.

Scarr, S., & Weinberg, R. A. (1983). The Minnesota Adoption Studies: Genetic differences and malleability. *Child Development, 54,* 260-267.

Schaffer, J., & Lindstrom, C. (1990). Brief solution-focused therapy with adoptive families. In D. Brodzinsky & M. Schechter (Eds.), *The psychology of adoption* (pp. 240-252). New York: Oxford University Press.

Schechter, M. D. (1960). Observations on adopted children. *Archives of General Psychiatry, 3,* 21-32.

Schechter, M. D. (1970). About adoptive parents. In E. J. Anthony, & T. Benedek (Eds.), *Parenthood: Its psychology and psychopathology.* Boston: Little, Brown.

Schechter, M. D., & Bertocci, D. (1990). The meaning of the search. In D. Brodzinsky & M. Schechter (Eds.), *The psychology of adoption* (pp. 62-92). New York: Oxford University Press.

Schechter, M. D., Carlson, P. V., Simmons, J. Q., & Work, H. H. (1964). Emotional problems in the adoptee. *Archives of General Psychiatry, 10,* 37-46.

Schmidt, D. M., Rosenthal, J. A., & Bombeck, B. (1988). Parents' view of adoption disruption. *Children and Youth Services Review, 10,* 119-130.

Seglow, J., Pringle, M. K., & Wedge, P. (1972). *Growing up adopted.* Windsor, U.K.: National Foundation for Educational Research in England and Wales.

Shapiro, M. (1956). *A study of adoption practice: Vol 1. Adoption agencies and the children they serve.* New York: Child Welfare League of America.

Sharma, A. R., McGue, M. K., & Benson, P. L. (1996a). The emotional and behavioral adjustment of United States adopted adolescents: Part 1: An overview. *Children and Youth Services Review, 18,* 83-100.

Sharma, A. R., McGue, M. K., & Benson, P. L. (1996b). The emotional and behavioral adjustment of United States adopted adolescents. Part 2: Age at placement. *Children and Youth Services Review, 18,* 101-114.

Shireman, J., & Johnson, P. (1986). A longitudinal study of black adoptions: Single parent, transracial, and traditional. *Social Work, 31,* 172-176.

Siegel, D. H. (1993). Open adoption of infants: Adoptive parents' perceptions of advantages and disadvantages. *Social Work, 38,* 15-23.

Silber, K., & Dorner, P. M. (1990). *Children of open adoption.* San Antonio, TX: Corona.

Silver, L. B. (1970). Frequency of adoption in children with neurological learning disability syndrome. *Journal of Learning Disabilities, 3,* 10-14.

Silver, L. B. (1989). Frequency of adoption in children and adolescents with learning disabilities. *Journal of Learning Disabilities, 22,* 325-328.

Silverman, A. R. (1993). Outcomes of transracial adoption. *The Future of Children, 3,* 104-118.

Silverman, A. R., & Feigelman, W. (1990). Adjustment in interracial adoptees: An overview. In D. Brodzinsky & M. Schechter (Eds.), *The psychology of adoption* (pp. 187-200). New York: Oxford University Press.

Silverman, A. R., & Weitzman, D. (1986). Non-relative adoption in the United States. In R. A. C. Hoksbergen (Ed.), *Adoption in world wide perspective: A review of programs, policies, and legislation in 14 countries.* Royesford, PA: Swets & Zeitlinger.

Silverstein, D. R., & Demick, J. (1994). Toward and organizational-relational model of open model. *Family Process, 33,* 111-124.

Simon, N. M., & Senturia, A. G. (1966). Adoption and psychiatric illness. *American Journal of Psychiatry, 122,* 858-867.

Simon, R. J., & Altstein, H. (1977). *Transracial adoption.* New York: Wiley.

Simon, R. J., & Altstein, H. (1987). *Transracial adoptees and their families: A study of identity and commitment.* New York: Praeger.

Singer, L., Brodzinsky, D. M., & Braff, A. M. (1982). Children's beliefs about adoption: A developmental study. *Journal of Applied Developmental Psychology, 3,* 285-294.

Singer, L. M., Brodzinsky, D. M., Ramsay, D., Steir, M., & Waters, E. (1985). Mother-infant attachment in adoptive families. *Child Development, 56,* 1543-1551.

Smith, D. W., & Brodzinsky, D. M. (1994). Stress and coping in adoption: A developmental study. *Journal of Clinical Child Psychology, 23,* 91-99.

Smith, D. W., & Brodzinsky, D. M. (1997). Coping with birthparent loss in adopted children. Manuscript submitted for publication.

Smith-Garcia, T., & Brown, J. S. (1989). The health of children adopted from India. *Journal of Community Health, 14,* 227-241.

Sokoloff, B. Z. (1993). Antecedents of American adoption. *The Future of Children, 3,* 17-25.

Sorosky, A. D., Baran, A., & Pannor, R. (1975). Identity conflicts in adoptees. *American Journal of Orthopsychiatry, 45,* 18-27.

Sorosky, A. D., Baran, A., & Pannor, R. (1978). *The adoption triangle.* New York: Doubleday.

Spitz, R. A. (1945). Hospitalism: An inquiry into the genesis of psychiatric conditions in early childhood. *Psychoanalytic Study of the Child, 1,* 53-74.

Sroufe, L. A., & Waters, E. (1977). Attachment as an organizational construct. *Child Development, 48,* 1184-1199.

Stein, L. M., & Hoopes, J. L. (1985). *Identity formation in the adopted adolescent.* New York: Child Welfare League of America.

Steinhauer, P. D. (1983). Issues of attachment and separation: Foster care and adoption. In P. Steinhauer & Q. Rae-Grant (Eds.), *Psychological problems of the child in the family* (2nd ed.). New York: Basic Books.

Stern, D. N. (1985). *The interpersonal world of the infant: A view from psychoanalysis and developmental psychology.* New York: Basic Books.

Stolley, K. S. (1993). Statistics on adoption in the United States. *The Future of Children, 11,* 26-42.

Talen, M., & Lehr, M. (1984). A structural and developmental analysis of symptomatic adopted children and their families. *Journal of Marital and Family Therapy, 10,* 381-391.

Talen, M. R., Pinderhughes, E. E., Groze, V., Swarztman, J., & Chen, M. (1997). Acknowledging difference in adoptive families: Helpful or harmful for adoptive family functioning? Manuscript submitted for publication.

Thompson, L. A., & Plomin, R. (1988). The sequenced inventory of communication development: An adoption study of two- and three-year-olds. *International Journal of Behavioral Development, 11,* 219-231.

Tizard, B. (1977). *Adoption: A second chance.* New York: Free Press.

Tizard, B., & Hodges, J. (1978). The effect of early institutional rearing on the development of eight-year-old children. *Journal of Child Psychology and Psychiatry, 19,* 99-118.

Tizard, B., & Rees, J. (1975). The effect of early institutional rearing on the behavior problems and affectional relationships of four-year-old children. *Journal of Child Psychology and Psychiatry, 16,* 61-74.

Toussieng, P. W. (1962). Thoughts regarding the etiology of psychological difficulties in adopted children. *Child Welfare, 41,* 59-65.

Verhulst, F. C., Althaus, M., & Versluis-den Bieman, H. J. M. (1990). Problem behavior in international adoptees: II. Age at placement. *Journal of the American Academy of Child and Adolescent Psychiatry, 29,* 104-111.

Verhulst, F. C., Althaus, M., & Versluis-den Bieman, H. J. M. (1992). Damaging backgrounds: Later adjustment of international adoptees. *Journal of the American Academy of Child and Adolescent Psychiatry, 31,* 518-524.

Verhulst, F. C., & Versluis-den Bieman, H. J. M. (1995). Developmental course of problem behaviors in adolescent adoptees. *Journal of the American Academy of Child and Adolescent Psychiatry, 34,* 151-159.

Wadsworth, S. J., DeFries, J. C., & Fulker, D. W. (1993). Cognitive abilities of children at 7 and 12 years of age in the Colorado Adoption Project. *Journal of Learning Disabilities, 26,* 611-615.

Ward, A. J. (1991). Prenatal stress and childhood psychopathology. *Child Psychiatry and Human Development, 22,* 97-110.

Warren, S. B. (1992). Lower threshold for referral for psychiatric treatment for adopted adolescents. *Journal of the American Academy of Child and Adolescent Psychiatry, 31,* 512-527.

Weil, R. H. (1984). International adoption: The quiet immigration. *International Migration Review, 18,* 280-281.

Weiss, A. (1985). Symptomatology of adopted and nonadopted adolescents in a psychiatric hospital. *Adolescence, 19,* 77-88.

Weiss, A. (1987). Reactions of mental health professionals to hypothetical clients: A comparison based on clients' adoptive status. *Psychotherapy, 24,* 414-420.

Westhues, A., & Cohen, J. S. (1990). Preventing disruption of special needs adoptions. *Child Welfare, 69,* 141-156.

Whiting, R. A. (1988). Therapeutic rituals with families with adopted members. In E. Imber-Black, J. Roberts, & R. Whiting (Eds.), *Rituals in families and family therapy.* (pp. 211-229). New York: Norton.

Wieder, H. (1977). On being told of adoption. *Psychoanalytic Quarterly, 46,* 1-22.

Wierzbicki, M. (1993). Psychological adjustment of adoptees: A meta-analysis. *Journal of Clinical Child Psychology, 22,* 447-454.

Winkler, R. C., Brown, D. W., van Keppel, M., & Blanchard, A. (1988). *Clinical practice in adoption.* New York: Pergamon.

Work, H. H., & Anderson, H. (1971). Studies in adoption: Requests for psychiatric treatment. *American Journal of Psychiatry, 127,* 948-950.

Wrobel, G. M., Ayers-Lopez, S., Grotevant, H. D., McRoy, R. G., & Friedrick, M. (1996). Openness in adoption and the level of child participation. *Child Development, 67,* 2358-2374.

Wulczyn, F. (1994). Drug-affected children in foster care in New York City. In R. Barth, J. Berrick, & N. Gilbert (Eds.), *Child welfare research review* (pp. 146-184). New York: Columbia University Press.

Yarrow, L. J., & Goodwin, M. S. (1973). The immediate impact of separation: Reactions of infants to a change in mother figure. In L. Stone, H. Smith, & L. Murphy (Eds.), *The competent infant.* New York: Basic Books.

Yarrow, L. J., Goodwin, M. S., Manheimer, H., & Milowe, I. D. (1973). Infancy experiences and cognitive and personality development at 10 years. In L. Stone, H. Smith, & L. Murphy (Eds.), *The competent infant.* New York: Basic Books.

Zill, N. (1985, April). *Behavior and learning problems among adopted children: Findings from a U.S. national survey of child health.* Paper presented at the meeting of the Society for Research in Child Development, Toronto.

Author Index

131

Subject Index

ABOUT THE AUTHORS

David M. Brodzinsky is Associate Professor of Developmental and Clinical Psychology at Rutgers University, where he also serves as Director of the Foster Care Counseling Project. Since receiving his doctorate in Developmental Psychology from the State University of New York at Buffalo, he has published widely in areas of child development and clinical psychology, with particular emphasis in the past 18 years on the adjustment of adopted children and their families. He has a private practice in South Orange, New Jersey, where he works primarily with members of the adoption triangle. He also is frequently called upon to serve as a forensic psychologist and expert witness in family law cases involving contested adoptions, child custody, and child abuse.

Dr. Brodzinsky has served as a consultant to numerous public and private adoption agencies and has conducted workshops on psychological issues in adoption and foster care for mental health and child welfare professionals throughout the United States, Canada, and Great Britain. He also currently serves on the Board of Directors of the Evan B. Donaldson Adoption Institute in New York City. His publications include *The Psychology of Adoption* (1990), edited with M. Schechter; *Being Adopted: The Lifelong Search for Self* (1992), with M. Schechter and R. Henig; and *Lifespan Human Development* (1993), with A. Gormly.

Daniel W. Smith is Assistant Professor of Clinical Psychology at the University of Arkansas. His current research and clinical interests focus on the assessment and treatment of child sexual abuse victims, as well as children's adaptation to adoption. He earned his doctorate in clinical psychology at Rutgers University, where he specialized in the adjustment of adopted and foster children. His experiences in working with the foster care system sparked his interest in the effects of child maltreatment, which he pursued during his internship and NIMH-funded post-doctoral training at the Medical

University of South Carolina's National Crime Victims Research and Treatment Center. He serves on the Editorial Board of *Child Maltreatment,* and is a frequent journal reviewer in the area of traumatic stress. He also co-founded the Children's Safety Center, the first multi-disciplinary child advocacy center in Northwest Arkansas.

Anne B. Brodzinsky is on the faculty of the Training Institute in Infant Mental Health in Newark, New Jersey and is a psychoanalytic candidate in the Child and Adolescent Program at the National Institute for the Psychotherapies in New York City. She has been involved in research and clinical work in adoption and foster care for the past 18 years. She has published widely on issues related to children's understanding of and adjustment to adoption, and recently has been pursuing research on the adjustment of birthmothers. She received her doctorate in counseling psychology from New York University.

Dr. Brodzinsky has served as a consultant to numerous public and private adoption agencies and has conducted workshops on the psychology of adoption for mental health and child welfare professionals, as well as for adoptive parents, throughout the United States and Great Britain. She has a private practice in South Orange, New Jersey, which is focused on members of the adoption triangle and is the author of *The Mulberry Bird* (1996), a well-known children's book on adoption.